Good Sports
Athletes Your Kids Can Look Up To

Good Sports

Athletes Your Kids Can Look Up To

Presented by Beckett Publications

Published by: Beckett Publications
15850 Dallas Parkway
Dallas, Texas 75248

ISBN: 1-887432-62-0

First Edition: August 1999

Beckett Corporate Sales and Information
(972) 991-6657

Jacket design: David Timmons
Front jacket photo: Tim Mantoani
Back jacket photos: Bill Baptist/WNBA (Cooper),
Peter Read Miller (Davis), Jed Jacobsohn/Allsport
(Sosa)

Book design: Hespenheide Design

Contents

Introduction

Don't hate Charles Barkley; he knows not what he says.

When Barkley goes before the world and proclaims, "I am not a role model," he doesn't understand that, in many ways, that's exactly what he is. Sure, Barkley's no saint, but the All-Star forward sets an example year after year as an individual who works very hard to be the best at what he does. And when Barkley represents the league at a charity function, such as the Houston Rockets' yearly Sunshine Kids trip for children stricken with cancer, he shows that some things are more important in life than simply drawing a paycheck.

No doubt, Barkley's argument is a compelling one. In his 1992 autobiography, "Outrageous!" Sir Charles addresses at length the subject of whether athletes are role models, and much of what he writes makes quite a bit of sense.

"If the only qualification for being a role model is that you have to be able to dunk a basketball, then I know millions of people who could become role models," Barkley writes. "That's not enough . . . I know drug dealers who can dunk. So can drug dealers be role models, too? . . . I also blame the parents who don't teach their kids proper values, and who don't tell their kids that respect and success in life have nothing to do with material wealth."

If all athletes and coaches were uneducated, non-caring, non-sharing robots, then Barkley's argument would leave no room for debate. But many athletes — certainly many featured in this book — have worked very hard and overcome many obstacles to become the highly paid celebrities they are today. Many had role models of their own who helped them achieve their success. And many want to pass on the lessons they've learned to other generations. Those are the athletes and coaches we've pinpointed for "Good Sports."

When setting out in search of 30 individuals who truly deserved the mantle of "Good Sport," we never used infallibility as part of the criteria. Some of the featured athletes have dabbled in the world of drugs, while others have made headlines for the success they've had in overcoming poor decisions or personal failures.

But these athletes did, at one point or another, have to make a difference in people's lives.

Perhaps that meant setting an example through hard work and dedication. That certainly would describe baseball iron-man Cal Ripken Jr., two-time WNBA Most Valuable Player Cynthia Cooper, world champion figure skater Michelle Kwan and hockey Hall of Famer Mario Lemieux.

Or perhaps that meant displaying

Mario Lemieux's body wasn't always willing, but his drive and determination went unquestioned.

courage through the toughest of times. Hall of Fame running back Walter Payton, battling the disease known as primary sclerosing cholangitis, certainly fits that bill. So does NASCAR driver Ernie Irvan, who miraculously returned to the top of the sport of auto racing after being given just a 10 percent chance of living following a crash in 1994. Other athletes found their way onto our list for their commitment to education. So next time your child tells you so-and-so didn't have to stay in school, point to NBA All-Stars Tim Duncan and Grant Hill or Heisman Trophy winner Ricky Williams. Many athletes earned our respect, and a place on our list, for their tireless charitable efforts. Sammy Sosa, Troy Aikman, and the aforementioned Mr. Hill know a little something about giving back to the community. (We've provided a list of many of the athletes' charities and their addresses on Page 128, so you can learn more about these worthy causes, if you choose.)

But regardless of the reasoning behind why these standouts were chosen, we think you'll be inspired by their stories, and by the all-encompassing photos that portray these athletes doing what they do best. So next time Mr. Barkley or another superstar proclaims it isn't his or her place to serve as an example to your children, don't fret. Just sit back, thumb through the pages, and see what makes these individuals athletes your kids can truly look up to.

Jim Abbott

First and Foremost, a Pitcher

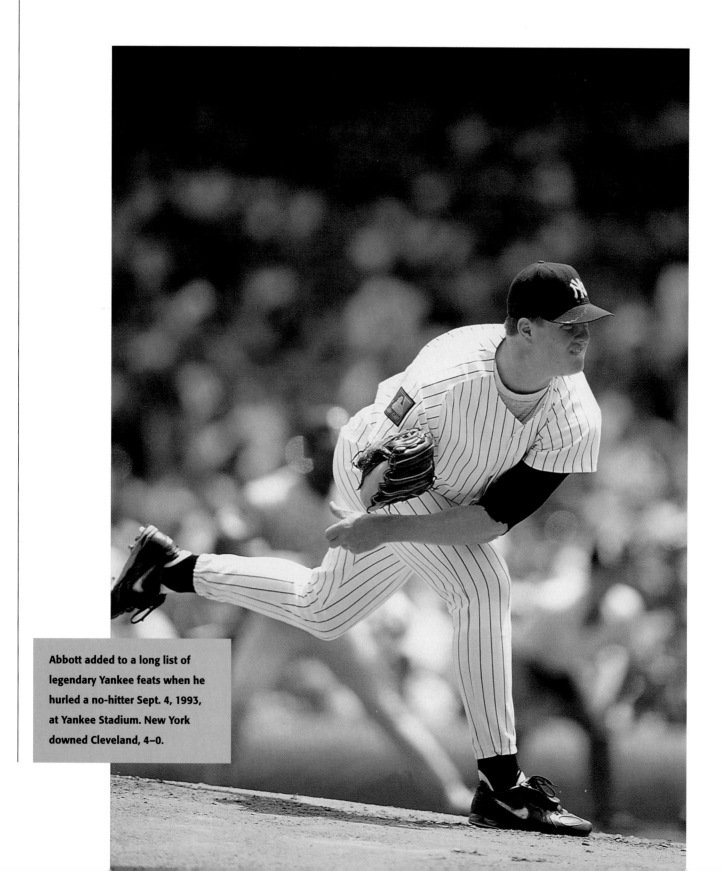

Abbott added to a long list of legendary Yankee feats when he hurled a no-hitter Sept. 4, 1993, at Yankee Stadium. New York downed Cleveland, 4–0.

Abbott was drafted by the Angels, with the eighth overall pick of the 1988 free-agent draft. He wasted little time thrilling Anaheim fans, becoming the first of nine pitchers who debuted in the majors to notch double figures in wins (12) his rookie season.

Flip over a Jim Abbott baseball card and marvel at his impressive litany of achievements:

- Jim was just the 15th player in major league history to go straight from a college diamond to the big leagues.
- At 22, Abbott was a starter in the Anaheim Angels' rotation and his name was on the lips of every baseball fan in the nation.
- He was an Olympic hero, winning the gold-medal game for the U.S. in the 1988 Games against Japan, and he claimed the Gold Spikes Award in 1987 as college baseball's premier player.

- In high school at Flint (Mich.) Central High, Abbott starred at quarterback and was first drafted in the 1985 amateur draft by the Toronto Blue Jays.
- He instead chose to attend the University of Michigan, where he studied communications and majored in striking out Big 10 opponents. He posted 82 Ks in 97.2 innings during his final collegiate season in 1988.
- As a member of the vaunted New York Yankees' rotation, Abbott hurled a no-hitter on Sept. 4, 1993, at Yankee Stadium in what was one of

In a Baseball America fan survey following the 1993 season, Jim was named the fifth-best role model in the Major Leagues.

Jim's ability to hit and field, in addition to strike out opposing hitters, has made it easy for fans to overlook his handicap.

the most cherished events ever staged at this historic ballpark.

Oh yeah, Jim Abbott also was born without a right hand.

Today, after more than a decade in the majors and a roller coaster career in his rear view mirror, that unbelievable sentence is no longer the headline

in Abbott's baseball life. The fact that fans actually boo Abbott following disappointing performances, which have become more frequent in recent years, is a testament to Abbott's ability to be accepted as a mainstream ballplayer despite a handicap that would have stopped most from even trying.

When one talks of athletes who inspire others to excel, Abbott's name tops everyone's list. How could he not be your hero? How could you not cheer for his every strikeout and every victory? Pitching in the big leagues is a fine art in which only the best of the best are allowed entry. Jim Abbott, who's fastball at its peak hit the low 90s, mastered this art with the type of determination and courage rarely displayed in any occupation.

Of course, Jim always knew that he'd be in the limelight because of his well-publicized handicap. In fact, he used the cameras, the reporters and the fame to his advantage by focusing the attention away from him and on other handicapped people, mostly kids, who also were achieving greatness.

There's no doubt that players such as Ken Griffey Jr., Chipper Jones and Cal Ripken Jr. receive more fan mail. However, how many of those letters are from children who've been inspired to walk for the very first time? And while Abbott no longer is a major league superstar, he remains and probably always will remain a fan favorite in whatever uniform he pitches.

Will he someday have a bust in the baseball Hall of Fame? It's unlikely. But in the Good Sports Hall of Fame, Jim Abbott is a first-ballot shoo-in.

Abbott was simply dominating during his college career at Michigan, posting a 26–8 career mark. In 1997, the left-hander received USA Baseball's Golden Spikes Award. In 1998, he was awarded the Sullivan Award, honoring the nation's top amateur athlete.

Troy Aikman

Your Friendly Neighborhood Cyberman

The phrase "larger than life" often is applied to superstars such as Troy Aikman. It's meant to illustrate how immensely popular an athlete or entertainer has become with his or her fans.

In Dallas, the phrase fits Aikman like a snug pair of shoulder pads. Since arriving in Big D from UCLA as the No. 1 overall selection and designated franchise savior in 1989, Troy has owned the city. After bringing home three Super Bowl trophies to his football-crazed town, the blue-and-silver No. 8 looms as large as the massive hole in the roof at Texas Stadium. Only Michael

Jordan in Chicago, Joe Montana in San Francisco and John Elway in Denver rival Aikman's remarkable acclaim in their own backyards.

But "larger than life" takes on a much different, much more significant meaning when applied to Troy's true passion: children.

The moment he inked his first mega-million dollar pro contract with the Cowboys, he started searching for appropriate ways to help the ones who needed it most. His first book, an autobiography, was not the typical athlete ego-feeding trite about how it felt to

Perhaps this childhood pony ride helped convince father Kenneth to move the family to the one-horse town of Henrietta, Okla., where Troy quickly became an athletic standout.

Aikman's charitable ways stop just as soon as he steps on the football field. The Cowboys signal caller, winner of three Super Bowls and one Super Bowl MVP Award, owns the NFL's third-best career completion percentage (62.0).

Troy took time out following one training camp session in Austin, Texas, to provide this young entrepreneur with some free publicity.

advantaged children in the Dallas-Fort Worth area. His unique End Zones, technology driven interactive play areas, were at the center of much of the funds. Each End Zone is set up with numerous computers that allow kids who ordinarily find it difficult to walk down the hall to travel the globe via the Internet. The battle zone is the isolationism each of these young people face each day.

Plugging into the Internet comes second nature to Aikman, who often travels the information superhighway to escape the limelight that his position in life brings. When a seemingly harmless trip to the grocery store can turn into a full-blown riot, sitting in front of the computer and meeting people on chat groups under an alias is a smart alternative.

Making wise decisions is what Troy does best. In the pocket, the strong-armed quarterback can pick a defense apart with his laser-beam passes. On the field, he's an intense competitor willing to give up body parts for first-down yardage. Although most quarterbacks would sacrifice their left arm (except maybe southpaws Steve Young and Mark Brunell) for three world championship rings, Aikman has said he often feels as if he missed an opportunity for more thanks to the chaos that's defined the Jerry Jones Cowboys era.

The Michael Irvin controversy was a true test for Aikman. While the evidence against his favorite receiver and good friend was overwhelming, Troy remained supportive and even showed up at one of Irvin's court hearings when other teammates kept a low profile.

During Barry Switzer's reign of terror, Aikman rarely enjoyed his job, and it showed. Despite his age, he contemplated retiring. But his mood

score the winning touchdown or sign the richest contract. Instead, it was targeted at kids with Aikman as the narrator of his own life decisions, both the good and bad ones. It was a best seller.

In 1992, he established the Troy Aikman Foundation, which benefits dis-

changed with a coaching switch —
Chan Gailey took over for Switzer in
1998 — and now Troy looks good to go
for at least another four to five seasons.

When he does finally retire, he no
doubt will be revered as one of the all-
time greats, a quarterback who was
"larger than life" on the field and off.
For thousands of kids who realize nothing or no one is larger than life, Troy
Aikman is just a friend. And that, more
than any touchdown pass or Super
Bowl MVP trophy, is a legacy Aikman
would like most.

**Troy announces the opening of Aikman's End
Zone, a computer area for kids with long-term
illnesses, at Children's Hospital in Oklahoma
City, Feb. 23, 1999. Brian Hess, a patient, gives
Troy his assessment.**

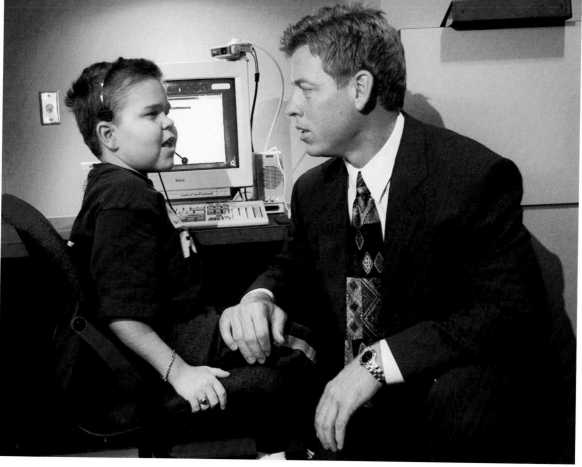

Cris Carter

Life's Lessons Learned

Cris, an ordained minister, gives praise following a playoff score against the 49ers on Jan. 3, 1998.

When Cris isn't busy tending to the Carter-White Charitable Foundation or working with Big Brothers & Sisters, he often speaks to schoolchildren about drug awareness.

Cris Carter has risen from the depths of NFL futility to the top echelon of the game. He has graduated from student to teacher in the process.

Carter's early NFL career appeared promising on the field, but somewhat shady off it. The young man who was convicted for defrauding his university in an agent scheme, succumbed to drug use and was even released from his first NFL team, now ranks as one of the league's premier receivers.

Carter evaded going to jail when he was placed on probation for concealing a payment made by sports agents before the 1986 season. Carter also pleaded guilty to obstructing justice when he concealed the payment from federal officers.

"I was concerned not so much with what the judge thought, but with what God would think," Carter said following his sentencing.

Carter showed flashes of brilliance in three seasons with the Philadelphia Eagles, but the character inconsistencies and tension with head coach Buddy Ryan caused the team to waive their talented project. The Vikings picked up Carter for a mere $100.

Since that low point, Carter has turned the thing around. He's grasped his faith as an ordained minister.

"I try to be steady as far as my walk every day and let people see God in me," he told ESPN The Magazine.

Carter's daily walk includes working with the Carter-White Charitable Foundation he co-founded with NFLer William White as well as the Big Brothers & Sisters program. Carter received the NFL's Extra Effort Award for outstanding commitment to

The Vikings took a chance in drafting troubled receiver Randy Moss, and with Carter's guidance, the rookie blossomed into the NFL's Offensive Rookie of the Year.

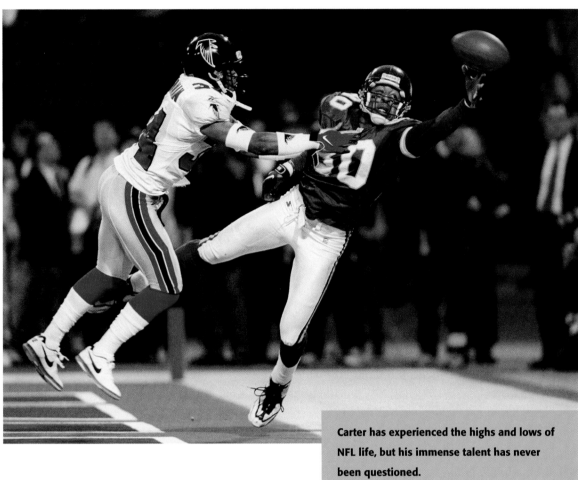

Carter has experienced the highs and lows of NFL life, but his immense talent has never been questioned.

community service activities in 1994 and was given the Athletes in Action Bart Starr Award in 1995. He frequently speaks to students on drug awareness.

Carter also has extended his mentorship to his teammates. His most publicized relationship has been with the NFL's 1998 Offensive Rookie of the Year, Randy Moss.

Moss possessed enough potential to be the first pick of the 1998 draft, but his checkered past caused him to drop late into the first round before the Vikings took a chance on him. Many observers believe that Carter's presence as a role model made the move pay off for the Vikings.

After being drafted, Moss went to work near Carter's Florida home, running, lifting weights and just talking. The role came easily to Carter, who regularly provides extremely blunt

cautionary speeches to incoming rookies as part of the NFL's newcomer program. Moss was no different.

"We talk a lot about personal issues as well as football issues," Carter said. "It's pretty simple: I want Randy to be a better receiver and have a better career than I have had. That was — and is — my sole motivation."

While Moss has taken a huge step early in his NFL career, Carter's huge career numbers in touchdowns and receptions will be hard to surpass. Even if Moss does manage to top Carter's numbers some day, he'll have a long way to go to match the future Hall of Famer's talents in helping other players reach their personal and professional potential.

Cynthia Cooper

A Champion's Cause

The world's most lauded woman basketball player is used to breaking down stereotypes and opening fans' eyes. Whether emerging from a crime-ridden neighborhood in Los Angeles as a youth, relocating to Europe to maintain her career choice, taking on the world in the Olympics, or taking a new pro league on her back as its best player, Cynthia Cooper doesn't know what it's like not to have a challenge in front of her.

Cynthia's latest challenge is her hardest. She must now carry the women's basketball torch without her mentor, role model and best friend. Despite the loss of her mother to a lengthy battle with breast cancer, Cynthia has decided to go on. To go after another WNBA title. To go after another WNBA Most Valuable Player Award. To go on breaking more ground for the women's game.

Cynthia has realized success around the globe and equated that success with her mother's presence and support. Her mother, Mary Cobb, was always there. If not in person, she was just a phone call away after each game.

Cynthia's achievements are impressive — two WNBA championships and MVP Awards, a gold medal in Seoul and two NCAA championships at USC — but none of these would have been possible without the drive and sacrifices her mother made for her and seven other children.

Cooper's unbreakable bond with her mother was witnessed by millions during the Houston Comets' two title

Cynthia, who shared a special bond with mother Mary, contemplated retirement after Mary died of breast cancer in 1999. But realizing that she couldn't in good conscience shirk her responsibilities, Cooper renewed her role as tireless supporter of the women's game.

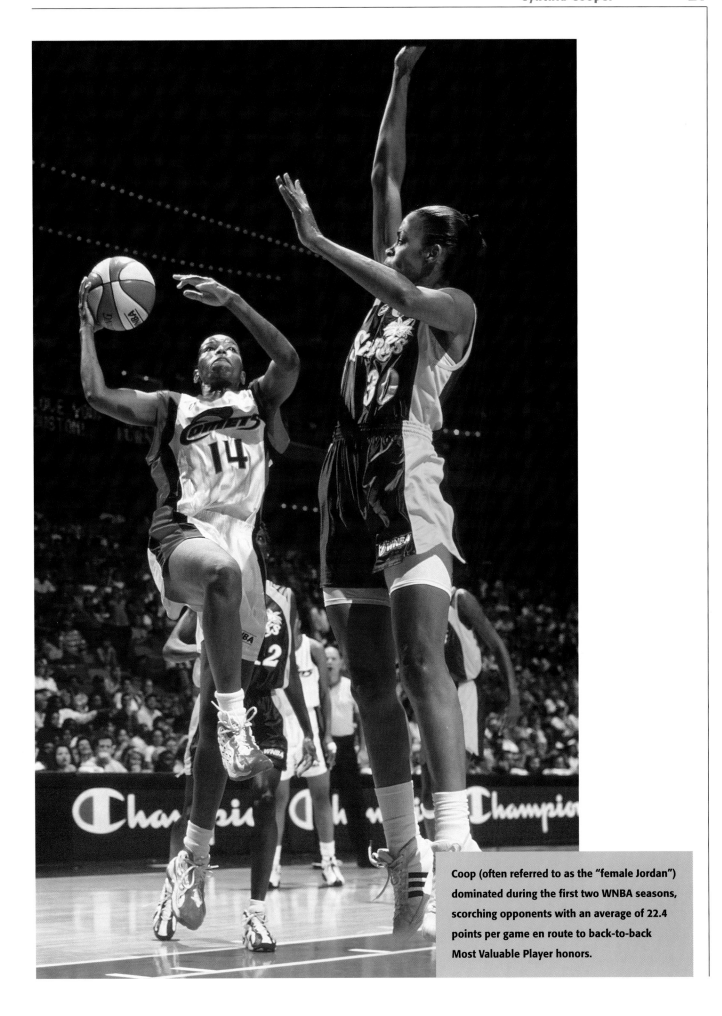

Coop (often referred to as the "female Jordan") dominated during the first two WNBA seasons, scorching opponents with an average of 22.4 points per game en route to back-to-back Most Valuable Player honors.

runs. Mary always was in the stands and in Cynthia's heart.

"I've got to be honest, a few weeks ago when my mother passed away, I did think about hanging them up," Cooper told ON Sports. "I just didn't know if I could play with the passion that I've always had. I was just so drained mentally and physically after spending so much time at her bedside in the hospital. I just needed some time to work everything out."

Cynthia has a history of working things out successfully. When her dream to play basketball for a living found no support in the United States, Cynthia took her game overseas. After 11 seasons in Europe and at the age of 34, Cooper came back home and became a pioneer for the WNBA women's basketball league. Cynthia has proven the perfect pacesetter in dealing with the league's growing pains and successes.

"There are plenty of sacrifices a pioneer must go through, but the bottom line is that it's worth it if women's basketball becomes successful in America," Cooper said. "That's the real reason I play this game. I want to make sure there's a future for American girls to play professional basketball in a league that respects their passion for the game."

You can hear her mother's influence come through in Cynthia's deter-

After helping to lead the USA to a gold medal in the 1988 Summer Olympics, Cynthia couldn't lift her fellow Olympians to gold in Barcelona in 1992. It was one of the few times Cooper, a member of two NCAA Championship teams and two WNBA Championship teams, suffered defeat.

Twice is nice: Cooper and the Comets dominated the Liberty, 65–51, to capture their first WNBA title in 1997, then served up a repeat performance with an 80–71 victory over the Mercury in the 1998 Finals.

mination to maintain her level of play and to become a role model like the woman who raised her.

"I figure I can play three to five more seasons at the level I'm at right now," Cynthia said. "And no one works harder at being a role model than I do. I believe it's part of my job and presents a rare opportunity to make a difference in young people's lives. I thrive on that privilege and plan on taking advantage of it for some time to come."

Terrell Davis

The ABCs of an MVP

He was the MVP of Super Bowl XXXII in January of 1998, and then of the entire NFL a season later.

He's one of just four men in history to ever rush for more than 2,000 yards in a single season, and he's improved upon all significant statistical categories in each of his four seasons, the last two of which ended with his team as world champions.

But there's more to Denver Broncos running back Terrell Davis

Terrell and mother Kataree have endured tough times, including an abusive relationship by Terrell's father and this brother's involvement in a deadly robbery.

Davis has emerged from the sixth round of the NFL Draft to become the most dominant rusher — if not the most dominant player — in the NFL. In 1998, Terrell became just the fourth player to rush for 2,000 yards en route to claiming NFL Most Valuable Player honors.

than hardware and hard work, although those qualities certainly have expedited his move to center stage.

Fact is, if you really want to know why Davis, TD to his teammates, is someone you and your kids can look up to, look no further than one of their favorite television shows, "Sesame Street."

That's right, ask Davis which he cherishes more, appearing on the late-night gab circuit with the likes of Jay and Dave, or doing the day-time gig with Elmo and The Count.

"A lot of people are asked to go on ["The Tonight Show with Jay Leno," "The Late Show with David Letterman"]

and shows like that," Davis told NFL Films late last season. "But how many players are actually asked to go on the "Sesame Street" show? Not many."

Then again, not many players are Terrell Davis, who wasted precious little professional time creating the Terrell Davis Salutes the Kids Foundation, an organization estab-lished to help children enjoy a better childhood.

Davis doesn't just accept the opportunity to reach young people. He covets it. Which is why, during the week prior to Super Bowl XXXII in his hometown of San Diego, Davis embraced the chance to impact the

Future Hall of Fame quarterback John Elway proclaimed Denver was now Terrell's team in the days leading up to Davis' MVP performance in Super Bowl XXXII.

student body of Lincoln High School, his alma mater.

The Cliffs Notes version of what he told the students who sat on the edge of their seats in the same gymnasium Davis himself once occupied, was this: Never lose sight of your dreams. Trite, you say? Well, then you don't know the speaker. And you probably don't know about the countless hardships he overcame growing up, practicing then what he preaches now: keeping one eye trained on your dreams.

Among the most compelling obstacles that littered his path to superstardom:

- Davis suffered even as a youth from the excruciatingly painful migraines that followed him into the early stages of his NFL career.
- Terrell's father once lined Davis and three of his five brothers up against a wall and fired a few warning shots from a handgun, just above their heads, as a means of teaching toughness.
- Davis' father died of lupus when TD was just 14.
- Davis spent four days in jail as a college freshman when he and a buddy tag-teamed the theft of four new rims for TD's car.
- Terrell's older brother, Bobby, single-handedly changed the American justice system when, during the course of an attempted robbery in San Diego, he killed the victim's unborn child.
- After Terrell's freshman season at Long Beach State, his head coach, the legendary George Allen, died, spelling the eventual demise of that school's football program. Terrell went on to finish his college career at Georgia and endured an off-again, off-again relationship with then head coach Ray Goff.

The point is, Davis overcame each of those obstacles, learning something from every one and always looking to the first lady in his life, mom Kateree, for assistance.

The finished product stands before us now as the best in his business, certainly on the field, and likely off it.

In April, Davis testified in front of Congress, supporting the need for more parks and athletic fields in urban areas.

"All children should have the opportunity to play sports and learn the valuable lifelong lessons that I was fortunate to have received," Davis told the Energy and Natural Resources Committee.

You see, Davis can do more than just tell you how to get to Sesame Street; he can tell you there needs to be a field or park on that street, too. For where there's a place to play, there's a chance for another Terrell Davis.

And that's good.

Terrell's toughness on the field is supplanted by a soft heart off it. Case in point: the running back's forming of the Terrell Davis Salutes the Kids Foundation, which focuses on improving children's lives.

Tim Duncan

"Good . . . Better . . . Best"

Tim Duncan didn't start playing organized basketball until he was a ninth grader, but his remarkable skills and good mental attitude quickly brought him up to speed with his peers, and then some.

By the time he was a freshman at Wake Forest University, he was accomplished enough that he started every game except "Senior Night." His sophomore year, in which Wake Forest won the Atlantic Coast Conference (ACC) Tournament title and claimed a No. 3 national rating, he earned All-America and All-ACC honors. By his junior year, when he led the Wake Forest Deacons to their second straight league title, he set a conference record for rebounds (56 in three games), averaged 22.7 points and 18.7 rebounds in the conference tournament and finished third in voting for the Wooden Award.

He also made, during his junior year, a decision that set him apart from a trend growing among other spectacularly talented young players. Rated a sure-fire No. 1 NBA Draft pick for 1996 if he decided to turn pro before graduation, Duncan decided to wait and return for his senior year at Wake Forest. Remembering a promise his father had made to his mother before she died, that all her children would finish school, Duncan decided to complete both his senior year and his degree in psychology.

"I felt that my time (for finishing school) was the present," Duncan told ON Sports in 1998. "I had to fulfill my promise, and no money in the world could have prevented that from happening. Looking back, I know I made the right decision."

Right decision, indeed. Not only was it a sound long-term decision in terms of completing his education, but it made possible a remarkable final year of college basketball and helped him hone his skills for what already has become a spectacular professional career. Besides the slew of awards Duncan won pronouncing him the top college player was a unanimous vote for the second year in a row to The

Duncan's athletic future appeared to be in swimming until Hurricane Hugo destroyed his local pool in the Virgin Islands.

Focused on his goals, Duncan averaged 21.1 points and 11.9 rebounds his first season and was the runaway winner of the Rookie of the Year award.

Dunkin' Duncan avoided the dreaded sophomore slump in 1998–99 and elevated his game to an even higher level, claiming NBA Finals MVP honors en route to leading the Spurs to their first-ever championship.

Associated Press All-America First Team. Not since Shaquille O'Neal had anyone repeated as the AP's unanimous choice.

Duncan also, of course, earned the undying gratitude of Wake Forest alumni, as well as fans of exciting college basketball everywhere.

Naturally, the NBA hadn't gone away, either, and in the spring of 1997

Duncan watched from the Virgin Islands (he grew up in St. Croix) as the San Antonio Spurs announced him as the first pick of the NBA Draft.

Praised on all sides as a future NBA star and key player for the Spurs, who needed another big man take the pressure off their star, David Robinson, Duncan managed not to let the talk of team "savior" go to his head. "I didn't know what to expect coming here," said Duncan in an interview with ESPN. "I knew there would be a lot of good players. The league is the best there is. Hopefully, I just wanted to fit in and find my way through it."

So modest was Duncan coming into the NBA that he agreed, upon the recommendation of Spurs head coach and general manager Gregg Popovich, to play in a summer league for rookies and free agents. Highly sought-after players with bigger egos might never have agreed.

Duncan's rookie season was a smash as he helped the Spurs put their disastrous 1996–97 campaign behind them and win the 1998 Rookie of the Year Award as well as earn a spot on the All-NBA First team. Despite putting up rookie numbers that could match any tried-and-true veteran's (he averaged 21.1 points and 11.9 rebounds per game), Duncan was very much a team player, not a showboat.

"He's not impressed with himself when he does something that's astounding. He's not depressed when he makes a mistake," Popovich told ESPN. "He just keeps competing. He's got no MTV in him at all. Tim Duncan just wants to get better."

And better he's gotten. In March 1999 he led the Spurs in scoring 14 times and in rebounding 10 times as the Spurs caught fire. Duncan and the Spurs ripped through the playoffs,

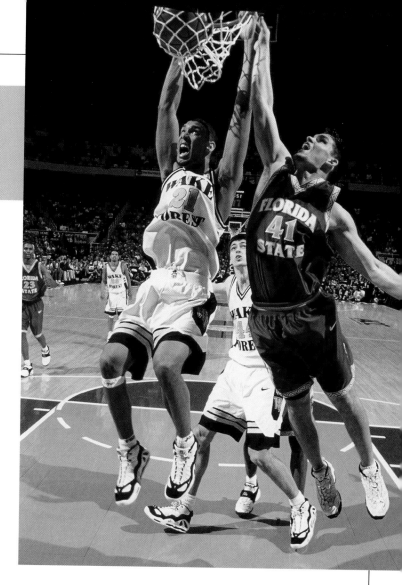

sweeping Portland and the L.A. Lakers before demolishing the Knicks, 4–1, in the NBA Finals.

Duncan seems to credit his mother for his success. She may never have taught him the fine points of basketball, but she drilled into him the importance of always doing your best.

"Good . . . better . . . best . . . never let it rest — until your good is better and your better is your best," Tim said. "I can remember repeating this line over and over for my mother as I was growing up in St. Croix. This is a motto never to be forgotten by any of my family. The lesson my mother taught me will always hold true."

As part of the NBA's Team Up program, Tim and his teammates work with South Texas middle schools to encourage students to get involved through community service.

Doug Flutie

When Miracles Happen

Doug Flutie's tradition of beating the odds began with a single unforgettable pass.

All hope had nearly faded away. Just seconds remained in the game, and it appeared as if Boston College's upset bid over the defending national champion Miami Hurricanes on Nov. 23, 1984, had fallen short. Trailing by four,

It all started with a single pass: Doug leaps into brother Darren's arms after throwing a last-second "Hail Flutie" touchdown pass to help Boston College shock defending national champ, Miami, in 1984. The throw solidified his choice as the Heisman Trophy winner.

the Golden Eagles were 48 yards from the end zone and had time for only one play. But Flutie was their quarterback and he still believed.

In an all-out scramble as the clock ticked near zero, Flutie desperately heaved a long bomb toward the goal line. Somehow, the ball arced over the Canes' blanket defense and dropped softly into the hands of Eagles receiver Gerard Phelan as he fell to the end zone turf. The 48-yard touchdown completion instantly silenced the Orange Bowl crowd and triggered a mad celebration among the visitors from the Northeast as Boston College knocked off Miami, 47–45.

It was a most improbable play in an improbable upset . . . and Flutie engineered it.

Though Flutie won the Heisman Trophy that year after setting the NCAA's all-time passing record, no one gave the quarterback much of a chance to succeed at the next level, primarily because he couldn't stand 6-foot on his tip-toes. Flutie was drafted in the 11th round of the 1985 NFL Draft and played in just 22 games for two different teams in four seasons before taking his game north of the border.

Coaches and scouts could measure his height, but what they all underestimated was the size of Flutie's heart. Flutie turned his NFL disappointment into motivation. Through hard work

Flutie was the media's darling in 1998 after returning to the NFL, leading Buffalo to the playoffs and earning a spot on the AFC Pro Bowl squad.

and determination, the 5-10 Flutie developed into one of the best quarterbacks in Canadian Football League history. He won six Most Outstanding Player awards and three Grey Cup Championships during his eight-year stint in the CFL.

Then, in 1998, Flutie returned to the NFL, signing with the Buffalo Bills as a free agent. After losing their first three games of the season, the Bills handed the reigns over to Flutie. And again Flutie delivered for his team. As the squad's starting quarterback, Flutie guided Buffalo to a Wild Card playoff berth and earned a spot on the AFC's Pro Bowl roster.

By continually beating the odds, Flutie has become a symbol of hope, encouragement and inspiration for all people trying to accomplish lofty goals. Families with members suffering from autism especially appreciate Flutie's work ethic. One such family is his own.

Three years ago, Flutie's only son, Doug Jr., was diagnosed with autism, a neurological and developmental disorder that affects a person's ability to communicate and reason. In April of 1998, Flutie and his wife, Laurie, developed the Doug Flutie Jr. Foundation for Autism.

"At first, it was hard to take, but we have to accept Dougie for who he is," Flutie says on the foundation's Web site, www.dougflutie.org. "He always has a smile on his face, and when he walks into a room, he brings a smile to your own face. He has many qualities about him that are special."

The Flutie family has established three primary goals for the foundation:

- To provide funding for services for financially disadvantaged families who need assistance in caring for their autistic children.
- To fund research and education into the causes and consequences of childhood autism.
- To serve as a clearinghouse and communications center for new and innovative programs and services developed for autistic children.

Through the Fluties' tireless efforts, and a popular cereal called "Flutie Flakes," more than $1 million was raised for the foundation in a little more than one year.

Flutie's generosity extends beyond the foundation for autism. He recently extended a hand to former fellow NFL quarterback, Jim Kelly, whose infant son, Hunter, suffers from a terminal illness called Krabbe Disease. The Doug Flutie Jr. Foundation for Autism donated $12,500 to Hunter's Hope, a charity organized by Kelly and his wife, Jill.

"Knowing as we do the pain and difficulties of having a child born with a medical condition, we wanted to help others in a similar situation," Flutie says on his foundation's site. "We also know that the challenges my wife, Laurie, and I have had having an autistic child pale in comparison to the difficulty Jim and Jill face, having a child born with an incurable disease."

Flutie also recently joined other top-notch professional athletes such as Nomar Garciaparra, Derek Jeter and Mia Hamm in the Fleet All-Star program. The Fleet organization is a community service initiative under which Flutie will make personal appearances and assist in community projects.

So why does a guy who's already defied the odds on the football field spend so much time trying to beat life's odds as well? Perhaps it's because Flutie knows as much as anyone that with hard work, compassion, humility — and a little luck — miracles can happen.

Flutie says Doug Jr., diagnosed three years ago with autism, "always has a smile on his face." Thanks to the Doug Flutie Jr. Foundation for Autism, and the phenomenally popular "Flutie Flakes," other families with autistic children receive financial support.

Jeff Gordon

Nice Guys Finish Fast

Gordon picked up a $1 million No Bull bonus for his victory in the Brickyard 400 in 1998, just a small contribution to the more than $20 million in prize money Gordon has accumulated in his short career. Much of the earnings, as well as money generated from memorabilia auctions, finds its way to charities funded by Gordon's Racing For a Reason foundation.

Who said nice guys always finished last? Jeff Gordon is such a nice guy that many NASCAR fans can't stand him. Of course, most wouldn't care about what a great guy Jeff is except that he wins 25 percent of his races and finishes in the top five more than half the time.

The three-time Winston Cup champion is one of those lucky guys who have it all, including the ability to polarize stock car racing fans. Half of the fans worship Gordon as the greatest driver of all time, while the other half boo him as a lucky upstart fortunate enough to be teamed with a great crew chief in Ray Evernham and wealthy car owner in Rick Hendrick.

Fans who believe Jeff's success is a product of luck and deep pockets don't understand that Gordon has been paying his dues for years. He began racing when he was 5 and broke onto the NASCAR scene in 1993 at age 22.

Gordon doesn't make it easy on either side, giving God all the credit while at he same time giving back with hours and hours of charity work. The 27-year-old has enormous talent, Hollywood good looks, more than $20 million in prize money, endorsement deals with major companies such as Pepsi and Frito Lay, and a beautiful wife. Not to mention the support of the best crew chief and team owner in stock car racing.

"People say I've been blessed, that I've had things easy," Jeff says. "But they don't know about how I grew up, how when I was a boy we'd drive from one race to the next, work on our own cars and sleep in the back seat. But they

Gordon rarely takes credit for his own success, often giving props to crew chief Ray Evernham, car owner Rick Hendrick, and the Man upstairs.

are right about one thing: It's been a dream come true."

Jeff's NASCAR career has indeed been a dream. Gordon won Winston Cup Rookie of the Year honors in 1993. The next year, he won two races and finished eighth in the points. In 1995,

Gordon broke out, winning seven races and his first Winston Cup title. At age 24, Jeff became the second youngest champion in NASCAR history.

In 1998, Gordon turned in perhaps the greatest season in NASCAR history. His 13 victories tied Richard Petty's

1975 mark as the most by any driver in a single season in the modern era (since 1972). At one point, Gordon tied another NASCAR record by winning four races in a row. Gordon scored 26 top-five finishes in all last season, including a staggering 17 in a row, and 28 top-10 efforts in 33 races. His 5,328 points set a record for the modern point system initiated in 1975.

The title was Gordon's third Winston Cup championship in four years; just two other drivers in NASCAR history have won more titles. But Jeff doesn't wage all of his battles on the track.

Gordon and Evernham have formed a non-profit foundation called Racing For a Reason that distributes money to charities. The two get their corporate connections to contribute, making the foundation a strong force.

Racing For a Reason also constantly runs fund-raising auctions on the Internet, with some top motorsports memorabilia up for grabs.

Gordon and his teammates are strong supporters of bone marrow transplants as well, since their owner Hendrick had to undergo one while battling leukemia. (Evernham's son, Ray J, also has been stricken with leukemia.) Gordon has been involved in many efforts to register potential donors and to raise money for research.

Do the boos bother Jeff? Isn't he tempted to quit the public charity work and go silent with his praise of God, just so he won't be a sitting target for the naysayers?

"I take the boos as the ultimate compliment," Gordon says. "That means we are winning. We hope to give them reasons to boo us for a long time."

Cammi Granato

Woman Among Boys

The San Jose Sharks' Tony Granato, a former member of the U.S. Olympic hockey team at the Calgary games, perhaps paid the ultimate tribute to his sister, Cammi, on the eve of her team's Olympic gold medal performance in the '98 Nagano games. "She's not my sister," he told Michael Farber from Sports Illustrated WomenSport magazine. "I'm her brother."

Tony, a former Olympian and member of the San Jose Sharks, says Cammi is the best hockey player in the Granato family. Cammi also is arguably the best analyst, serving as the Los Angeles Kings' color commentator.

He wasn't just being polite, either, a gracious older brother deferring to his sister's time in the limelight. He was telling the world, subtly, just whom it was in the Granato family deserving of top billing when it came to hockey skills.

Consider Farber's own assessment of Cammi's abilities: "She is not the fastest skater nor does she have the industrial-strength shot, but she has an innate sense of the game and passes as well as almost anyone who isn't named Gretzky. She is the best American women's player and one of the Top 5 in the world, which gives her a status more like that of Pat LaFontaine, Chris Chelios or Brian Leech than that of, say, Tony Granato."

Unfortunately for Cammi Granato, women's hockey is one of the more undeveloped sports in this country. There are few players (less than 22,000, according to Farber, as recently as 1997), no professional venues, and little possibility of an image-building event such as the faceoff between Billie Jean King and Bobby Rigg that gave rise to women's tennis in the '70s. After all, it's not likely that a team of middle-aged men's hockey players are going to take on Cammi and her Olympic teammates at Caesar's Palace on national TV.

Then again, who knows? The Olympics victory marked a watershed for women's hockey, and a few years

Cammi's passing ability and general feel for the game sets her apart from other hockey players.

ago, there was no such thing as women's professional basketball, either.

Certainly there were no organized hockey teams for girls when Cammi (given name, Catherine Michelle Granato) was growing up in suburban Chicago. No matter. She played with her three older brothers and she played, from kindergarten on, with a boys team, the Downers Grove Huskies. Resisting all attempts by family and outsiders alike to give up hockey for something more conventional, such as figure skating, she played on, putting up with the inevitable episodes of hostility that seem to erupt when girls invade "boy sports."

Not until she started at Providence College did Cammi play with an all-women's squad. And it was at Providence that she led her team to back-to-back Eastern College Athletic Conference Championships in 1991–92 and 1992–93. She completed her college career as Providence's all-time leading goal scorer.

If women's hockey gains mainstream acceptance, supporters will have Cammi, captain of the gold medal-winning U.S. team in Nagano, to thank.

Granato joined the U.S. Women's National Team when it began in 1990 and became its leading scorer. Captain of the U.S. team at Nagano, she led the Americans to a thrilling win over the Canadian team in the first-ever Olympic-sanctioned women's games. Throughout the games she acted as ambassador for women's hockey, doing the promotion that's necessary for an emerging sport and encouraging girls worldwide to follow their muse, wher-

Cammi and her USA teammates were picture perfect at the Nagano games, overcoming a tough challenge from the Canadians, 3–1, to win the first-ever women's ice hockey gold medal.

ever it led them. "Young girls should believe in themselves and feel confident in their abilities, she said in an interview with Electra magazine. "Women can go a long way, but you have to dream big and don't feel afraid to make a mistake."

If the Olympic victory over the tough Canadians, and the acclaim that followed it — a Top 10 gig on David Letterman, a Wheaties box appearance, a Nike endorsement, and lots and lots of interviews — was the peak of her career, it also made her realize there was a valley looming below. What to do now? With no hockey equivalent of the WNBA, Cammi had nowhere to go in the hockey world, regardless of her acclaim.

The solution: a new job as a broadcaster with the Los Angeles Kings. It may not be perfect, but her job as radio color analyst has kept Granato in touch with the sport (she often scrimmages with the Kings on ice before games and conducts hockey clinics in the L.A.

area.) It also keeps her in the spotlight, plugging away as a role model for girls.

And while there are the same kinds of complaints she's encountered all her life about playing where she doesn't "belong," she keeps a level head and looks to the future.

As she told the Canadian Press about her feelings when people call in to complain about her role in the booth: "You never know if it's an attack on you personally or if it's an attack on you as a woman. I've found that all my life, but I could back it up. I could step out on the ice and run around people. In broadcasting, I'm starting out at the beginning. Any woman who has succeeded had to break down some barriers."

Cammi already has won over her talented brother, and no doubt, many of the fans who watched her lead the U.S. squad in its quest for the gold in Nagano. And if Cammi continues to champion her sport, nationwide acceptance for women's hockey may not be far behind.

Adam Graves

Selfless Devotion

Adam Graves isn't the sort of guy who likes to talk about himself.

Ask him about scoring a franchise-record 52 goals in 1993–94 with the New York Rangers, and he says he wishes he could cut the puck used for the historic final goal into 25 pieces to thank his teammates.

Ask him about helping the Rangers end their 54-year Stanley Cup drought in 1994, or his first Cup with the Oilers in 1990, and he immediately defers credit to those around him in the dressing room.

Ask him about his selfless devotion to community service, and he'll deflect praise as easily as he does a low, hard shot from the point. "I just consider myself fortunate," he'll say simply.

Adam Graves may be a great hockey player. But he's a far better person.

"I don't think he really realizes how much people look up to him," former junior teammate and best friend Glen Featherstone told the New York Times. "Adam's the kind of guy that, if he picked up garbage for a living, he'd still be doing charity [work]. It's not about [feeling some kind of responsibility] as a hockey player. It's about what kind of person he is."

> "Adam's the kind of guy that, if he picked up garbage for a living, he'd still be doing charity [work]. It's not about [feeling some kind of responsibility] as a hockey player. It's about what kind of person he is."
> — Glen Featherstone, former teammate

Many accolades have been bestowed upon Adam Graves — both because of his immense hockey skills and his tireless devotion to charitable causes.

Graves, who shared his childhood home with more than 50 foster children, always is willing to lend an ear — or a quick hockey lesson — to New York-area kids.

Selflessness is a lesson Graves learned early in life. Growing up in North York, Ontario, a suburb of Toronto, Graves shared his home and his parents' love with more than 50 foster children.

"We were all treated the same," Graves told Sports Illustrated. "We shared everything. I never felt that my mum or my dad loved these kids any less than they loved me or my two biological sisters."

A lot of kids would have had problems with this arrangement. Not Adam. The newcomers, typically troubled children from abusive backgrounds, were welcomed as brothers and sisters. To this day, Adam thinks of every child who passed through the home as family.

Graves may be the perfect example of the nice guy finishing first. After being selected by the Detroit Red Wings in the second round of the 1986 NHL Entry Draft, Graves led his junior team, the Windsor Spitfires, to the Ontario Hockey League Championship and the Memorial Cup Finals in 1988.

Although he didn't flourish immediately upon entering the NHL the following season, Graves persevered. After brief stints in Detroit and Edmonton, he ultimately earned recognition as a Second-Team NHL All-Star in 1993–94 and appeared in his first All-Star Game that same season.

If he were the sort of guy who took satisfaction in individual acclaim, he'd probably be prouder still of winning the King Clancy Award that season, for leadership on and off the ice and contributions to the community. If it were possible to win the award multiple times, there's no doubt his quiet heroism would have forced the league to create another trophy to let other players have a chance.

"People sometimes get the impression that any kind of community work is all show with athletes," says former junior teammate Peter DeBoer. "Not Adam. He's always the first in line whenever anyone needs any help. He's so genuine. The amazing thing is, as much as you see him do, there's so much else he does that people never hear about. It's a priority with him."

Not that his on-ice efforts have suffered. After battling through a series of injuries and changing roles on the Rangers, Graves returned to the goal scoring charts in 1998–99, potting 38, good for 11th overall.

As pleasing as rediscovering his offensive touch — and a new three-year, $12 million contract with New York — must be, Adam remains refreshingly down to earth, and very cognizant of his responsibilities.

"I'm very fortunate," he told SI. "I had a mum and dad and a family when I was growing up. They taught me how to live. You try to teach others the same things.

"You know, I love hockey. I love to play the game, love everything about it, but it's not real [life] is it? Making sure kids feel wanted, making sure they grow up right, that's what's important."

We'd all be fortunate to remember that ourselves.

Mia Hamm

Move Over Betty

The poster, showing a young woman flying around a soccer field, carried a tagline that made you realize just how far the culture has come since the days of "Father Knows Best." The message: "Sugar and Spice and bone-jarring slide tackles, that's what little girls are made of."

Well, some little girls, anyway. Pretty many, come to think of it, in this era when girls' and women's sports have taken off in popularity, from the youngest kids playing grade school soccer to the legions of adult women participating in everything from radical freestyle skiing to ice hockey. The days of girls hanging out at the malt shop, waiting to be asked out by a boy and maybe trying out for the cheerleading team, seem to belong closer to the Victorian period than the recent past.

But that's the reality, and the girl pictured in the "Sugar and Spice" poster, soccer star Mia Hamm, has a lot to do with it. Hamm, as anyone who's seen her mobbed after a game knows, is an

Fans have become used to Mia's ability to score acrobatic goals — and then celebrate with style.

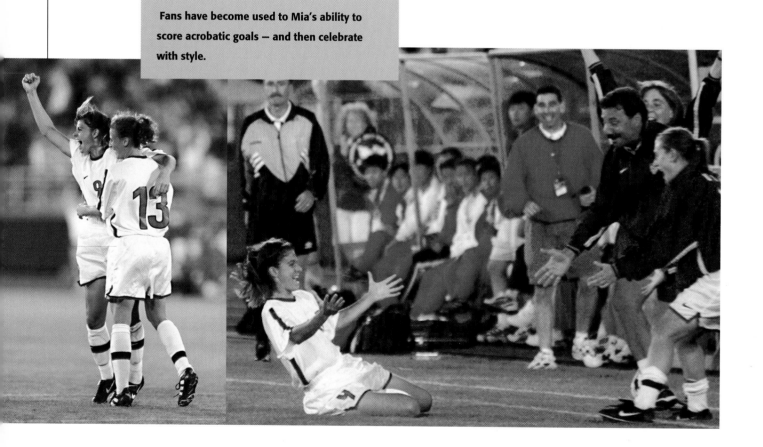

Hamm's physical toughness, coupled with an electrifying personality, makes her the perfect role model for young women athletes.

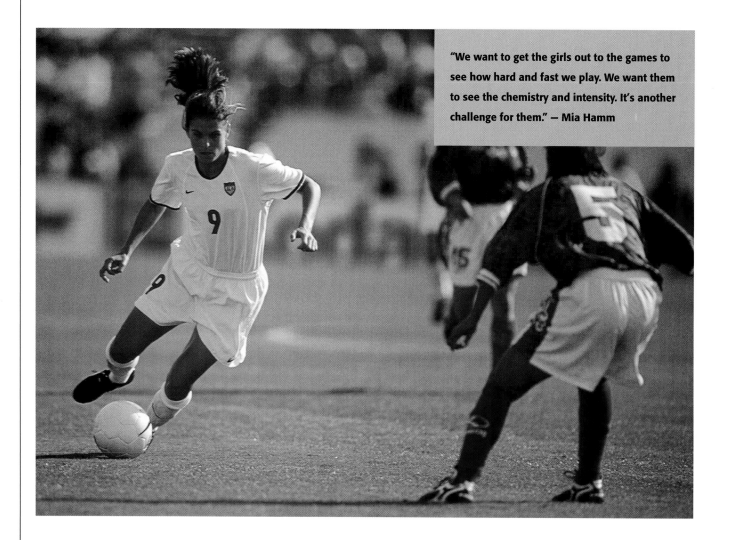

idol for young girls today. Forget using "Father Knows Best's" Betty Anderson as a role model. Today, it's the accomplished, aggressive doer, especially on the athletic field.

That's why Hamm was a perfect choice to play opposite Michael Jordan in Gatorade's "I Can Do Anything Better Than You Can" television campaign.

And as a doer, Hamm has packed a lifetime of accomplishment into her young years. Among her successes:

- Hamm's the all-time leading scorer in NCAA women's soccer with 103 goals and 72 assists.
- On Dec. 12, 1987, she became the youngest woman (15) ever to play for the U.S. National Team.
- She was MVP of the 1994 Chiquita Cup and the 1995 US Cup.

- As captain of the U.S. women's soccer team at the 1996 Olympics in Atlanta, a hobbled Hamm led her squad to the gold medal with a dramatic 2–1 victory before a record crowd.

And hey, she's pretty enough, too, to have rated a place on People magazine's list of the 50 Most Beautiful People of 1997.

Born in Selma, Ala., in 1972, Mariel Margaret Hamm was one of six children of Col. Bill Hamm, a career Air Force officer, and his wife, Stephanie. As a military brat Hamm grew up on the move, always playing a spectrum of sports. But it was soccer, which her father had grown to love while stationed in Italy, that she found most simpatico.

"I found I cared more about the results in soccer than in any other sports," she said in a 1997 interview with Sports Illustrated Women Sport. "It made me who I am. I was given a tremendous gift in terms of athleticism. I believe it was given to me for a reason. And maybe it was because I wasn't so confident in other areas."

By the age of 14 she was the dominant girl player in Texas; and at 15 she took her game to the highest of levels by joining the national women's team.

The rest — her four consecutive NCAA championships with the University of North Carolina, her NCAA records, her selection as Outstanding Female Athlete in all of college sports in 1994, the frenzy that erupted after she and her Olympic teammates won the gold, her endorsement deals with products ranging from Gatorade to Earth Grains, Pert Plus to Pepsi, and, of course, the inevitable Nike — was just waiting to happen.

Soft-spoken and shy, and anything but egotistical, Hamm is nonetheless a fierce competitor on the field. Off the field, though, the striker often called the best woman soccer player on the planet is quick to attribute her success to her teammates and is often mortified by the publicity she receives (especially the 50 Most Beautiful gig). But she goes along with it because she wants to promote both the game of soccer and the ideal of accomplishment for young girls.

"We want to get the girls out to the games to see how hard and fast we play," Hamm told WomenSport. "We want them to see the chemistry and intensity. It's another challenge for them."

She also plays, in a way, in memory of her older brother, Garrett, who had mentored her in the ways of soccer

Hamm watches as her international record-setting 108th career goal rips past goalie Didi and into the net during a 3–0 victory over Brazil, May 23, 1999.

when she was just starting to play. Garrett died during her team's Victory Tour in 1997 from complications resulting from a rare blood disorder. Despite her loss, she only missed two games.

"Garrett passed away, [and] there was no bitterness," Hamm told the Chicago Tribune. "He didn't want us to feel guilty. He knew we'd be sad, but he would want us to remember him most by going out and doing the things he couldn't do and the things we love to do."

For Hamm, and the throng of female fans in her wake, that means playing sports with reckless abandon.

Grant Hill

Moving Mountains

Take one look at Grant Hill's off-the-court resume and you'd think he's waging a one-man war on the NBA's much-deserved bad boy image.

For instance, enroll your kids in Hill's yearly basketball camp and the Detroit Pistons forward will see to it that they learn academic and social skills in addition to the fundamentals of hoops. Buy Hill's book, "Change the Game," and proceeds go to homeless children's organizations in New Orleans and Baltimore. Head to a Detroit-area park or playground, and there's a good chance that Hill's efforts helped build or maintain the area. Flip on the television, and you may catch one of Hill's Public Service Announcements on the National Safe Kids Campaign, Black History Month or the Newspaper Association of America.

And that's just the tip of the iceberg. When Hill's not striving to be the best all-around player in the NBA, he's

Taught that anything is possible through dedication, Grant has succeeded at the college, Olympic and professional levels.

"In those early days I thought my mom was so unfair. By the time I went to college though, I realized that she had given me a great tool [self discipline]." — Grant Hill

constantly using his superstar status to help others.

The 6-8 forward credits his famous parents for instilling in him compassion and a strong work ethic. Mother Janet, an attorney and consultant in the Washington, D.C., area, and father Calvin, a former NFL All-Pro running back, taught Grant that he could succeed at anything through dedication.

Hill's parents could be tough at times; no bad deed went unpunished. "In spite of what you may have heard, he was not perfect as a teen-ager and did get into trouble . . . [but] it was never serious, and he never got into trouble for the same thing twice," father Calvin said in 1996.

But Hill now has formed a special bond with his parents. He has recalled how his father's celebrity status and competitiveness pushed him to be a better person. He also has mentioned how he didn't enjoy his mother's insistence on childhood piano lessons, but now he rarely passes a baby grand without giving in to the urge to tickle the ivories.

"In those early days I thought my mom was so unfair," Hill said in "Change the Game." "By the time I went to college though, I realized that she had given me a great tool [self discipline]."

Well-rounded: On the court, Grant has led the Pistons in scoring, rebounding and assists for three consecutive seasons; off the court, Hill has won the Congressional Award Foundation's Horizon Award and has become a major supporter of Special Olympics.

Hill applied the lessons he learned from his parents on the court, helping to lead the Duke Blue Devils to back-to-back NCAA championships in 1991 and 1992. Opting not to leave school for the NBA early, and setting another example of the importance of education in the process, he graduated in 1994 with a B.A. in history.

Hill was an instant success at the next level, winning co-Rookie of the Year honors in 1994–95 and helping lead Dream Team III to a gold medal in the 1996 Summer Olympics. As a testament to his work ethic and well-rounded talents, he has led the Pistons in points, rebounds and assists for three consecutive seasons (1996–97 to 1998–99), becoming one of just three NBA players to lead their teams in all three categories more than once.

All the while, Hill, a winner of the Congressional Award Foundation's Horizon Award, honed his community service skills.

So if you contribute to Special Olympics, you can take comfort in knowing Hill is Vice-Chairman of the Board of Directors for the 1999 Special Olympics World Summer Games. And if you ever need Meals on Wheels, Hill could be dropping off your dinner during the holidays. And if . . . well, you get the picture.

Ernie Irvan

Rolling with the Punches

If anyone best represents the No Fear philosophy, it's Winston Cup driver Ernie Irvan. The comeback cowboy of auto racing, Irvan has stared death in the eye. And death blinked.

Irvan, in fact, does wear the No Fear brand. The driver is such a good friend of the Simo brothers, owners of the in-your-face apparel company, that the Simos have sponsored him and formed ownership teams with him. And when Irvan released his autobiography early during the 1999 racing season, the Simos gave him permission to use "No Fear" as the title.

Once known as "Swervin' Irvan" by his NASCAR comrades, Ernie has become a respected veteran driver.

Irvan recovered quickly from his near-fatal crash in 1994, climbing back into his No. 28 car late in the 1995 season and posting a pair of top 10 finishes.

Irvan grew up just a couple of miles away from Laguna Seca Raceway in California and fell in love with racing. As a young adult, Irvan decided to leave home with $300 and a map to North Carolina, the hub of stock car racing. A couple of years later he found himself welding grandstand seats at Charlotte Motor Speedway during the day and racing at nearby Concord (N.C.) Motorsports Park at night.

Irvan eventually made several Winston Cup starts for a variety of teams before getting his big break late in the 1990 season with the Morgan-McClure team. Ernie showed he had more than just potential, needing just 105 starts to capture nine poles and seven victories, including the 1991 Daytona 500.

Yet Irvan drew harsh criticism for his aggressive style, which often led to pinball-type incidents in which multiple cars went bouncing off everything in sight. His hard-charging approach earned him the nickname of "Swervin' Irvan."

Ultimately his style got him in trouble with his fellow NASCAR drivers. A couple of the sport's biggest names, legends Darrell Waltrip and Richard Petty, told him things had to change. So Irvan showed up at the drivers' meeting before a race in Talledega and apologized, promising to take a safer approach.

In 1992, following the untimely death of driver Davey Allison in a helicopter crash, Irvan took over behind the wheel of the famous No. 28 car of

Ernie Irvan's path to success hasn't always been sweet, but Irvan has endured. Now he and his No. 36 M&Ms car are NASCAR fan favorites.

Robert Yates Racing. Ernie immediately blossomed, collecting five wins, seven pole positions, 21 top-10 finishes and 18 top fives in just 29 starts.

Irvan was at the pinnacle of his sport when a tire went flat during a practice session at Michigan Speedway in August of 1994. The car, speeding along at nearly 200 mph, slammed into the outside wall, and in an instant, Irvan was critically injured.

Emergency crews raced to Irvin's aid. No major bones were broken but his heart and brain were bruised. Irvan's lungs collapsed, and he had fractures at the base of his skull. He lapsed into a coma and was given just

a 10 percent chance of living.

Remarkably, Irvan awoke from his coma in three days, and a year and several operations later, Irvan was back in the No. 28 car. The only visible sign of his ordeal: a patch over his left eye to compensate for blurred vision.

He proved he was ready by finishing in the top 10 twice in his three starts late in the 1995 season. He raced with Yates Racing for all of 1996 and 1997, with one of his three victories in those two years an emotional win at Michigan Speedway.

Irvan and Yates parted company in 1998 because the sponsor of his car wanted a new driver. But Irvan quickly

Irvan proved he could still stand the heat by winning a combined three races in 1996 and 1997, including the Jiffy Lube 300 (above) and the Michigan 400.

regrouped, signing with the MB2 team, and now drives the popular No. 36 car sponsored by M&M/Mars.

"I've been as high as you can get in this sport, and I've been as low as you can get," Irvan says. "And I've been a lot in the middle. The path on the way up is really, really hard. The path on the way down is like falling from a tree. The path even back to the middle is definitely hard.

"It's a tough sport."

But not too tough for Irvan, who's still standing after taking some of the best punches this unforgiving sport has to offer.

Michelle Kwan

Grace Under Pressure

For people not intimately acquainted with the world of women's figure skating, the first they heard of California wunderkind Michelle Kwan was when she appeared as an asterisk on the page of the Tonya Harding/Nancy Kerrigan Sturm und Drang of 1994.

With Harding under attack for whatever role she might have played in the knee-bashing of teammate Kerrigan, it was unclear whether Harding would be allowed to participate in the Olympic Games. Arriving in Norway as a possible alternate, and practicing on ice as if she

Kwan skated with elegance at the Nagano Games, then showed no ill feelings when younger Tara Lupinski walked away with the gold.

were to compete, was the young sensation Michelle Kwan.

In the end, of course, Harding was allowed to compete, her tear-filled problems with her laces winning her not a medal but only immortality in a famous Seinfeld sendup. For Kwan, who won her first competition at age 7,

Critics doubted Michelle Kwan's resolve at the 1999 World Figure Skating Championships, but a bad cold, commitments with Disney and college application anxiety probably had more to do with why Kwan was upset by Russia's Maria Butyrskaya.

the Olympics would have to wait. In the meantime, though, there were championships to be had.

She was a perennial winner or runner-up in competitions the next four years, among them the Goodwill Games, Skate Canada, Skate USA, U.S. Postal Service Challenge, Centennial on Ice, The Continents Cup, the Trophy Lalique, the Japan Open and the World Figure Skating Championships.

She was not merely victorious in her programs, but almost magisterial, her performances having a grace and beauty that gave another dimension to her athleticism. So accomplished was she that Kwan has received perfect 6.0 marks nearly 40 times in her career.

So when the Nagano Olympics opened in 1998, it was no surprise that Kwan was considered the favorite to take the gold. But it was not to be. Her teammate, the even younger Tara Lupinski, skated away with the ultimate prize, leaving Kwan with the second-place silver.

Expected to be devastated by the disappointment, she later claimed that it had not been the tragedy everyone imagined. "I don't think if I could go back in time, I would change anything," the Associated Press reported her saying during the 1999 Figure Skating Championships. "It helped me grow as a person and as an athlete. So I think it was good. It was meant to be. Right now, I feel I'm stronger than ever from the Nagano experience. It's helped me mature and pushed me further."

She would need the mental stamina. For, after winning the U.S. Competition, she suffered a disappointing defeat to Russia's Maria Butyrskaya during the World Championship soon afterward. Although she had arrived for the Helsinki competition suffering from a bad cold, commentators said her performances lacked their usual flair, artistry and emotion. Perhaps she was missing the competition that Tara Lupinski used to provide before she turned pro.

But for a woman with a lot on her plate — she was awaiting the results of her college applications to, among others, Stanford, UCLA, UC-Berkeley and Harvard, and was busily at work starring in new productions for the Walt Disney Co. — she seemed less worried about what the future held than many others.

"I'm just glad that it's not like skating is everything," Kwan was quoted in the Detroit Free Press. "It's not like if I don't win, I'm going to burst into flames."

"Right now, I feel I'm stronger than ever from the Nagano experience. It's helped me mature and pushed me further." — Michelle Kwan

Mario Lemieux

A Warrior's Courage;
A Gentleman's Class

The date: April 26, 1997. The event: a Pittsburgh Penguins-Philadelphia Flyers NHL game in Philadelphia. The outcome: a 5–3 loss by Pittsburgh and the last appearance by the great Mario Lemieux.

The sporting world wouldn't see a retirement to match its significance until the soft fading away of Wayne Gretzky in the spring of 1999.

In his final game, Lemieux got a goal and an assist, fitting last markers on a remarkable career that, in sports terms, anyway, was almost a walking Shakespearian tragedy. For if Lemieux was capable of performing almost superhuman feats in the rink — and the three-time NHL MVP and six-time scoring leader certainly was — he also was dogged by recurrent health problems, which kept him off the ice for large chunks of time. Through it all, though, Lemieux kept battling. And winning.

Mario Lemieux was born in 1965 in a small, working-class town outside Montreal, where hockey, as in so many parts of Canada, was worshipped as the only game. Having started skating as

The sight of Lemieux breaking loose on a one-on-one shootout was a goalie's worst nightmare. Mario exhibited the same tenacious drive in waging his own one-on-one battle with Hodgkin's Disease.

"If he hadn't gone through all the back problems and cancer, [Lemieux] might have been the guy who statistically could have shattered all my records. I mean all of them [including] 215 points, 92 goals." — Wayne Gretzky

early as age 2 or 3, he was playing hockey by the time he was 6. By 16 he was out of school, ready to concentrate on making hockey a career.

After playing with the Quebec Major Junior Hockey League (where he got an amazing 11 points his final game), he was ready for the NHL, becoming the first selection in the 1984 draft. Drafted by the also-ran Pittsburgh Penguins, it took him one game to get his first goal. By the end of the 1984–85 season, Mario had scored 100 points and was Rookie of the Year, and was well on the way to making the Penguins a viable team.

By the late 1980s, his reputation was made. In the 1987 Canada Cup

Lemieux scored the goal (on a pass from Gretzky) that broke a 5–5 tie with the Soviet Union and won the tournament for Canada. "Lemieux, who scored a series-leading 11 goals," said writer Larry Schwartz in an article for ESPN.com, "emerged from the Canada Cup a decidedly different young man. He had ripped up his reputation as someone who was lazy and lax when the going got tough and replaced it with the respect of the world's players."

Problems with his back, though, were already serious, though you would never guess the number of games he missed from looking at his points scored.

In the 1988–89 season Lemieux was able to play just 26 games, but he

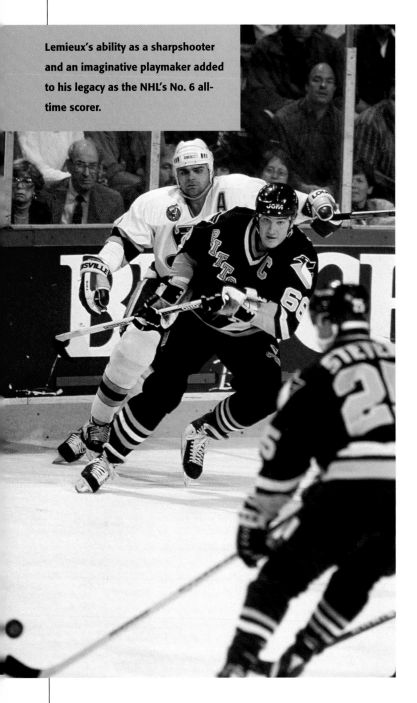

Lemieux's ability as a sharpshooter and an imaginative playmaker added to his legacy as the NHL's No. 6 all-time scorer.

record of 215 points. But he also encountered potential mortality when doctors discovered he was suffering from Hodgkin's Disease. Surgery and radiation therapy took care of the cancer but kept him sidelined for two months in 1993. A week after his return, though, he led his team on what was to become a record, 17-game winning streak.

After missing most of the 1993–94 season and all of 1994–95 because of back-related problems, he again returned to form in his last two seasons and retired, that momentous day in 1997, as the No. 6 all-time scorer in the NHL. Less than six months later, he was inducted into the Hall of Fame, bypassing the usual three-year waiting period reserved for lesser mortals.

Who knows what he would have done if all those missing games had been productive ones? As Wayne Gretzky said, "If he hadn't gone through all the back problems and cancer, he might have been the guy who statistically could have shattered all my records. I mean all of them [including] 215 points, 92 goals."

Despite false rumors of a return to the ice in 1998, Lemieux was still producing for Pittsburgh, buying the team that had fallen into bankruptcy proceedings in June 1999.

When asked how he wanted to be remembered, Lemieux said simply, "Just as somebody who took a last-place team and won a championship." But others were more perceptive, paying tribute to his character as a player and human being.

"Remember him for his gifts, his grace and beauty on the ice," said Howard Baldwin, the former Penguins owner who signed him to his big contract. "And most of all, remember his courage."

was there when Pittsburgh most needed him, playing brilliantly in the postseason to lead the Penguins to their first-ever Stanley Cup. More back problems the next season and even a broken hand suffered in the playoffs didn't keep Lemieux from winning his third scoring title and leading the Penguins to their second straight Stanley Cup.

Then came the year of greatest highs and lows: 1992. Mario signed a 7-year, $42 million contract, and it appeared as if he might beat Gretzky's

Mario Lemieux personified many positive values to Penguins' fans and the city of Pittsburgh. An NHL Hall of Famer. A source of civic pride. A champion on the ice and off. Lemieux took his final bow before the Penguins' home crowd during the 1997 Stanley Cup playoffs.

Casey Martin

A Cause Worth Fighting For

"I don't want them to take pity on me because I limp around. . . .You might as well chase your dreams while you're young before it's too late. I'm not going to let my leg stop me."
— Casey Martin

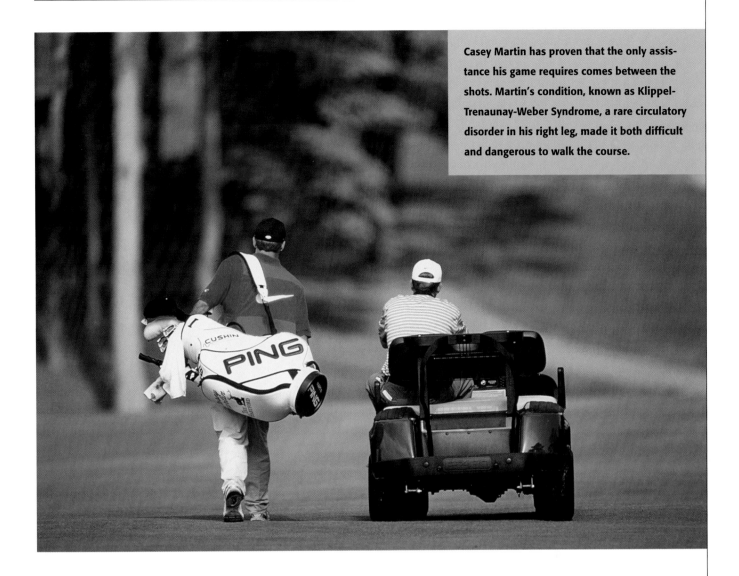

Casey Martin has proven that the only assistance his game requires comes between the shots. Martin's condition, known as Klippel-Trenaunay-Weber Syndrome, a rare circulatory disorder in his right leg, made it both difficult and dangerous to walk the course.

For a few weeks in early 1998, golfer Casey Martin was getting way more than his allotted 15 minutes of Andy Warhol fame. Martin, then a 25-year-old graduate of Stanford University with a rare circulatory disorder in his right leg, found himself in the awkward position, for a golfer, of having to sue the PGA Tour.

The issue was whether Martin's condition, known as Klippel-Trenaunay-Weber Syndrome, made it both difficult and dangerous to walk the course, and if so, whether he could have the use of a golf cart to travel the distance between holes. Martin's doctors claimed that too much stress on his withered right leg could cause it to break and necessitate amputation.

The PGA lawyers said that rules were rules, and the allowance of a cart for Martin was both against the sport's storied tradition and an unfair advantage over other golfers walking the entire course.

The debate raged on TV screens across the country. Was Martin merely attempting some sort of scam, thanks to a loophole provided by the Americans with Disabilities Act? (The ADA had never before been invoked for competitors in a major sport.) Or was he just one disabled person asking for a chance to be able to play?

Were the traditions and competitive balance of golf under attack, as PGA defenders such as Arnold Palmer and Jack Nicklaus testified? Or was the

Martin was ready to return his focus to golf after winning his case against the PGA in 1998 but was forced to return to the U.S. Appeals Court during the appeals process.

whole issue simply about accommodating a man with a medical condition?

"Believe me," said Martin before the trial, "I just want to be given a chance to play. I wouldn't have done this if I'd have thought I had an advantage [with a cart]."

In the end, Casey won his case, allowing him to compete in the PGA Tour with the use of a cart. In victory, he said that although he had taken on the PGA for his personal benefit, he knew that the larger issue was that his victory could be an inspiration for others with handicaps.

"I realized if I win, that would open the way," he said in a post-trial press conference. "That's something to feel good about. I'd like to be a role model. Hopefully, I'll do a good job."

The commercial and endorsement offers that had poured in even before the case was decided (Nike clothes, books, infomercials, Christian ministry, etc.) would help him get his message across. As Martin said in a Nike ad that was part of the sneaker giant's new "I Can" campaign: "I don't want them to take pity on me because I limp around. . . . You might as well chase your dreams while you're young before it's too late. I'm not going to let my leg stop me."

Above all, Martin seems free of self-pity, knowing that however difficult his medical condition, he still is able to lead a successful and productive life. As he told ESPN, who asked if doctors had told him how much longer he could expect to keep his leg, he said: "They've never said, 'You have 2.5 years left,' but

Martin knew that his legal campaign could be an inspiration for others with handicaps. "I realized if I win, that would open the way. That's something to feel good about. I'd like to be a role model. Hopefully, I'll do a good job."

they have said, you know, I'm on kind of a time bomb here.

"And that's fine. A lot of people deal with a lot worse than I do, so if I have to walk with a prosthesis, that's certainly not the worst thing in the world."

And Martin surely knows that should his golf career end tomorrow, his fame — however unintentional — and his gift for inspiring others would continue.

Mark McGwire

On Tators & Tot

They say he saved baseball. Perhaps, through his monumental feats both on and off the field, he's really saved much more than that. A sense of national pride . . . reassurance that today's world is going to be just fine, just as it was 40 years ago for Roger Maris, 70 years ago for Babe Ruth . . .

That is what Mark McGwire is all about.

He's had more than one chance to etch his name in stone in the record book. Back in 1987, his rookie season, McGwire entered the last game of the year with 49 home runs. The chance to hit 50 — such a nice, round number — was so close to his reach he could almost grab it with one of his huge, burly arms.

But McGwire never showed up. Seems he had more important matters

Mark McGwire's heroic traits had become front-row fodder well before he tied Roger Maris' home run record with this shot, his 61st round-tripper of the 1998 season.

It was a special day for McGwire fathers and sons. Not only did Mark celebrate his record-tying 61st home run with 10-year-old Matthew in grand fashion, but he also served up one heck of a gift for his own dad, John — the eldest was in the stands celebrating his 61st birthday.

McGwire has embraced Cardinal fans as much as they have cherished him. A portion of Interstate 70 in St. Louis was renamed I-Mac in honor of the historic slugger.

to attend to than attempting to become just the 12th player to bash 50 homers in a season. His son, Matthew, was born that day in Oakland, and the A's were playing on the road in Chicago. So much for No. 50. The record book would have to wait.

For 11 seasons it waited. Finally, in 1998, McGwire did the unimaginable: 70 home runs. That's five more than Matthew predicted he would hit before the season.

"I asked him how many home runs he wanted his dad to hit," McGwire said. "He looked me in the eye and said, 'sixty-five.' "

The road to 70 was not an easy one. There was a divorce from Matthew's mother, Kathy. The split was amicable, allowing Mark to remain close to his son. When McGwire signed with the Cardinals as a free agent, he made sure that his child would have a seat on the team plane when Matthew could go on road trips, and he made darn sure his son could work as a bat boy whenever he was able to attend home games.

There were injuries, and then more injuries, mostly of the nagging kind that don't go away quietly, without more pain. Who knows when McGwire could have broken the home run record if he hadn't missed all those games from 1990 to 1996?

There were sessions with a therapist that helped McGwire cope with it all. The slugger had developed a reputation among media members for not being the friendliest postgame interview. A divorce, and being thrust into superstardom at such an early age, can do that to a guy.

Then, he saved baseball. Heck, he probably saved a lot of us. Because of his remarkable on-the-field exploits, our country was introduced to Matthew, and we were told the story of a man, a very big man, who overcame a lot to achieve so much. A man who was a good father . . . a good person.

And in the midst of it all was Matthew. That's who was waiting at home plate when his father, after nearly missing first base in all the excitement, rounded the diamond after launching No. 70.

"He didn't have to say anything," says the elder McGwire. "His eyes said it all."

Whether it's at the ballpark playing catch or at the movie theater watching a film, Mark and his son, Matthew, cherish the time spent together. "He knows what his dad has done, but he just knows me as a dad," says the elder McGwire. "And that's the most important thing."

Despite fame and fortune, the modest McGwire avidly supports charitable causes, such as at this event in West Hollywood benefiting child literacy. During the 1999 season, for every home run that McGwire hits, Starbucks donates $5,000 to a children's charity in the host city where the game is played.

Paul Molitor

Respecting the Game

He was one of the game's greatest hitters — a 21-year veteran with a perfect swing. He's a member of the 3,000-hit club, standing with Ty Cobb and Honus Wagner as the only players ever to collect 3,000 hits, 600 doubles and 500 stolen bases. He was the MVP of the 1993 World Series; a man whose

More than two decades after grabbing American League Rookie of the Year honors, Molitor hung up his spikes following the '98 season. "I think I've done what I can do on the field in terms of fulfilling everthing I possibly could have dreamed of in major-league baseball," Molitor said. "It has been a great ride."

39-game hitting streak came the same year (1987) he hit a career-high .353.

For all his talent, he had spent most of his career in relative obscurity in small-market Milwaukee, playing for the Brewers for 15 years before going on to three-year stints with the Blue Jays and the Twins. Only in Toronto would he know the glories of victory in a World Series when he sparked his teammates to ultimate triumph with his 12-for-24 performance in the '93 Fall Classic.

And then, with a reluctant announcement at a press conference weeks after his final game in 1998, he was gone from baseball as an active player. It didn't have to be so, for he was still a valued commodity, with offers to return for another year from both the Brewers and the Blue Jays. In fact, both his wife and his agent had urged him to do just that, but in the end, the mild-mannered Midwestern veteran decided to take his 3,319 hits and call it a career. It wasn't easy for the man who had long hesitated to use the word "retire," who worried that once he was gone, he would really be gone.

"I don't know how to write an epitaph in terms of your playing days," Molitor said. "I hope that regardless of what they saw on the field that they saw a respect for the game and a passion for the game, and someone who was a good teammate. Some of those things

No matter what position he played — first, second, third, outfield or designated hitter — the "Ignitor" sparked his club with smarts, speed and a sweet swing. Molitor played the game to a purist's delight, respecting baseball's deep history and traditions.

It's only fitting that Molitor's 3000th hit on Sept. 16, 1996, was a triple. After the hard-nosed veteran motored into third base, the Metrodome speakers blared "Born to Run" by Bruce Springsteen, Molitor's favorite singer.

by the Cardinals, but opted for college first. Once in the game, his talents manifested themselves quickly, and he was named AL Rookie of the Year by The Sporting News in 1978.

Injuries plagued, but never derailed Molitor's career. He always came back, and he was always productive. In 1984, he played a career-low 13 games because of an elbow injury but bounced back the next year to hit .297 with 10 home runs, 48 RBIs and 21 stolen bases. Starting with his first time on the disabled list — about a month in 1980 — until retirement, he would miss

that hopefully talk more about character than performance."

It was both character and performance that were in evidence throughout a long career that started in 1977 with the Brewers. The St. Paul native had been drafted several years earlier

the equivalent of 500 games. That's three entire seasons.

He still, though, managed to pile up those 3,319 hits in 10,835 at-bats, finishing his time in baseball eighth in career hits and tied for 10th in doubles, with 605. Admirers could only wonder what kind of numbers he could have put up had he had some of those 500 games back to play.

However, Molitor wasn't just a good ballplayer. He was a good and generous teammate liked by both peers and fans — a community-minded man tireless in raising funds to combat AIDS and children's cancer.

Even a flirtation with cocaine in the 1981 season failed to damage his image with the fans. Not only had he always flown low on the radar screen of stardom, he just evoked that solid Midwestern image people couldn't help but like.

As Richard Hoffer said in Sports Illustrated in 1993, when Molitor was finally leaving Milwaukee to go to the Blue Jays, "He has been so low profile that even when he admitted to using cocaine in 1981, he was unable to cast off his image as the apple-cheeked all-American boy. . . . This is a guy who values modesty, privacy and restraint in all areas outside the ball-park."

Mercury Morris

Never Too Late

For a man who was an integral part of "The Perfect Team" — the undefeated, 17–0, Miami Dolphins of 1972 — life has seemed less than perfect. A stellar career in collegiate and professional football was followed by a long, hard fall, culminating in a conviction and imprisonment on charges of selling cocaine. And even when the conviction was eventually thrown out on appeal and he began a new career as a businessman, communicator and motivator, life went anything but smoothly for Eugene "Mercury" Morris, one of the great running backs in NFL history.

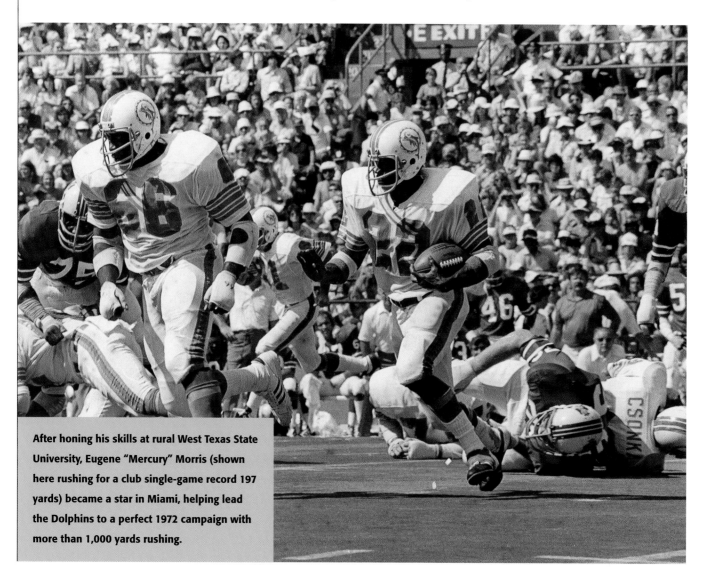

After honing his skills at rural West Texas State University, Eugene "Mercury" Morris (shown here rushing for a club single-game record 197 yards) became a star in Miami, helping lead the Dolphins to a perfect 1972 campaign with more than 1,000 yards rushing.

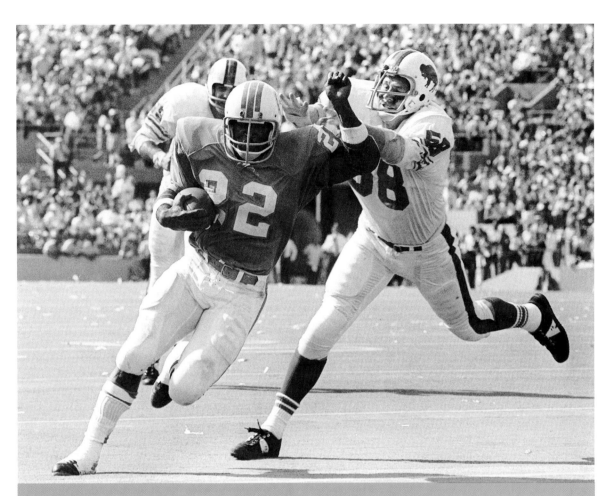

Dolphins fans chanted, "Go Merc. Give the ball to Merc," during Morris' heyday.

For years he turned up in the news pages involved in one dispute or another, many of which he attributed to pure and simple racism. Despite his problems, however, he has been consistent in trying to help others avoid the kinds of difficulties he created in his own life.

Born and raised in Pittsburgh, Morris first achieved notoriety on the football field at West Texas State University, where he was a record-setting fixture from 1965–1969. In the process of rushing for more yards than any other runner in the history of college football, Morris picked up the nickname "Mercury." He also picked up two All-America honors and a third-round draft invitation to join the Miami Dolphins.

Starting off his pro career as a kick return specialist with the Dolphins, Morris wasted no time gaining attention. On his first kick return, against the Cincinnati Bengals, he returned the kick 105 yards for a touchdown, which turned out to be the second longest in the NFL record book.

The day would be only the first of many highs to come, among them his selection to three Pro Bowl teams (the first being in 1971), the years-long rivalry with O.J. Simpson, and his 1,000-yards rushing gained during that perfect season of 1972. He was only the third Dolphin to ever achieve that plateau.

The best times came during the early '70s when the Dolphins, on their way to back-to-back Super Bowls, won

32 out of 34 games, including the 17–0 start for 1972. During those years the city and stadium rocked with joy, calling out, "Go Merc. Give the ball to Merc." It couldn't last, though, and it didn't. As time went on, Morris' shaky relations with head coach Don Shula deteriorated even more. And in 1976, he was traded to the San Diego Chargers, a bad team far from his Miami home.

It wasn't the makings of a happy new situation. And after a mediocre season in California, Morris called it quits on professional football.

Like many an athletic hero who had given much more thought to The Game than to any possible life After The Game, Gene Morris found himself adrift when the cheering had stopped. He developed both money troubles and physical troubles. Worse yet, casual drug use from his days as a player turned into full-blown cocaine addiction.

Morris' cocaine addiction led to his arrest in 1982 and subsequent trial on drug trafficking charges. He was sentenced to 15 years, and served three and a half years before the Florida Court of Appeals ruled the trial judged erred in not allowing a witness to testify, and his trafficking charges were dropped.

The bottom really fell out of his life, however, when he was arrested at his home in 1982 on charges of conspiracy and trafficking in cocaine. Morris admitted to being an addict, but vehemently denied dealing, and charged the government with entrapment. When a witness essential to his case was not allowed to testify, he was convicted and sentenced to a mandatory 15 years in prison. He served three and a half years before the Florida Court of Appeals ruled the trial judge had made an error in not allowing the witness to testify, and ordered a new trial.

Morris soon was out, his days as an undirected addict behind him. His wife said prison had been a good thing for him, making him a "a better husband, a more responsible father." With new purpose in his life, he hit the national lecture circuit hard, talking about his Christian conversion, his victory over drug addiction, and how he, and others, could turn adversity into triumph in life.

Nearly 20 years later, and now an executive involved in energy management, he's still at it, speaking regularly to groups ranging from business associations to kids in juvenile hall. The message? Success is possible for anyone, and adversity needn't be a permanent condition.

"What I speak about are possibilities." Morris told a typical crowd of seventh-graders in Miami a few years ago. "When you speak about what's wrong all the time, when you finish, all you have is what's wrong. If you don't speak about possibilities, you don't have it.

"One of the greatest things about school is that you invent who you are going to be. Who you are right now is a possibility, and all you are is a possibility. Where am I going to be in the next five years when I graduate high school? The only way you know that is to begin to plan it now."

Alan Page

Life & Order

Hall of Famer Alan Page was known as a fearsome competitor on the football field, a defensive tackle for the Minnesota Vikings and Chicago Bears whose skills were so exceptional that they not only terrorized quarterbacks but they came to revolutionize the very nature of his position.

But as far as Page was concerned, his 12-year career in the NFL was nothing more than a temporary diversion, a job that kept him busy while he waited for his real career to begin. A career that has led him all the way to the Minnesota Supreme Court.

Page was not the type of person to find himself wondering what he would do next. Partly because it is the Notre Dame graduate's nature to be prepared, and partly because he never defined himself as a football player, he was ready to move on when the time came.

When asked by a writer for Runner's World magazine why his Minneapolis home exhibited no football mementos, the nine-time Pro Bowl selection and 1972 Most Valuable Player said, "Well, I was a person before I was a football player. Football was something I happened to do. In my mind's eye, I never saw myself as a football player — not even when I was a little kid growing up in Canton. On the other hand, I do see myself in my mind's eye as a runner."

Alan Page, member of the famed "Purple People Eaters," was every offensive lineman's nightmare during his 12-year NFL career.

Page (pictured with fellow Purple People Eaters Jim Marshall, left, and Carl Eller, right) applied his strong work ethic in the legal profession, where he became an assistant state attorney general, and ultimately, a justice of the Minnesota Supreme Court.

Page and his Minnesota teammates never won a Super Bowl, but he left the game with no regrets.

Somewhere along the line, Page also must have seen himself as a lawyer and public servant, for, even before his days as a member of the famed Purple People Eaters were over, he was studying law at the University of Minnesota, poring over his books while other players partied. By 1978, he had his degree.

Returning to Minneapolis after his final NFL days with the Bears, he plunged into his post-football career. By 1985, he had become an assistant state attorney general dealing in employment litigation.

In 1992, he was elected to the Minnesota Supreme Court with 62 percent of the vote, becoming the first black to hold a statewide elective office and the first to sit on the state's Supreme Court. Typical for a man who had long exhibited an interest both in children and education, he invited 140 fourth-grade students to the ceremony.

"Success comes with hard work, it comes with preparation," Page said at the ceremony. "And when you do prepare, then you can achieve your hopes and dreams."

Besides his personal example of a life well led when it's marked by hard work and study, Page set up a structure — the Page Education Foundation — to help the disadvantaged achieve success, too. "It has a two-fold purpose," Page told the New York Times in 1995, when he was being inducted into the Pro Football Hall of Fame in his hometown of Canton, Ohio. "One, to motivate minority children academically beyond high school. Two, to provide financial aid to high school graduates.

"But as a requirement of receiving financial aid, a college student would be required to come back to the community and work with fourth-, fifth-, and sixth-grade students to impress upon them not only the importance of staying in school but also their education beyond that."

From only 10 scholarships awarded its first year in 1988, the foundation grew to the point where it handed out more than 300 scholarships by 1996. "Next to love, education is the most powerful and lasting gift we can

"In my mind's eye, I never saw myself as a football player. . . . On the other hand, I do see myself in my mind's eye as a runner."
— Alan Page

give to our children . . . [the recipients] have been given not only money, but encouragement . . . and hope . . . and a whole new world of choices," Page said in a speech to Kentucky Wesleyan College. "With apologies to Vince Lombardi, preparation isn't everything, it's the only thing."

Typical of Page's priorities and attitude toward life, when he was inducted into the Pro Football Hall of Fame, he chose as the person who would present him the bronze bust not some former teammate or coach, as most players do, but a high-school principal (Willarene Beasley) from Minneapolis. "The rea-

son is very simple," he told the New York Times. "To the extent that we portray athletes as heroes and role models, selecting a black educator will project a positive image, especially to disadvantaged and minority children. If the inductee is a role model, the presenter should be."

Even in Page's crowning moment of football glory, he couldn't help but look ahead.

Walter Payton

Playing for Keeps

"If there's a way to beat it, he'll beat it, and be a great example for anybody who gets in dire circumstances." — Mike Ditka

Long after the cheers at Soldier Field had subsided, Walter Payton, the great Chicago Bears running back, showed how much he remained a part of the collective Chicago consciousness. Appearing at a news conference on Feb. 3, 1999, the two-time NFL Player of the Year announced that he was suffering from a rare liver disease called "primary sclerosing cholangitis" and that he needed a liver transplant to save his life.

Chicago was, to put it mildly, stunned at the news, and erupted in an outpouring of support for the man who had come to town to play football and had stayed for a business career. Day by day after his announcement, the city tried to assimilate the news, and in doing so, learned more about the serious disease that had indiscriminately inflicted their NFL hero.

It was a hard situation to imagine Payton, a nine-time Pro Bowl selection, being in. After all, he was known as an iron man who played with pain, missing only one game in his 13-year career — and that one under strong protest.

He was strong. During his playing days, from 1975 to 1987, the Mississippi native could bench press 390 pounds and squat 640 pounds. In retirement, managing a business empire that included restaurants and nightclubs, an

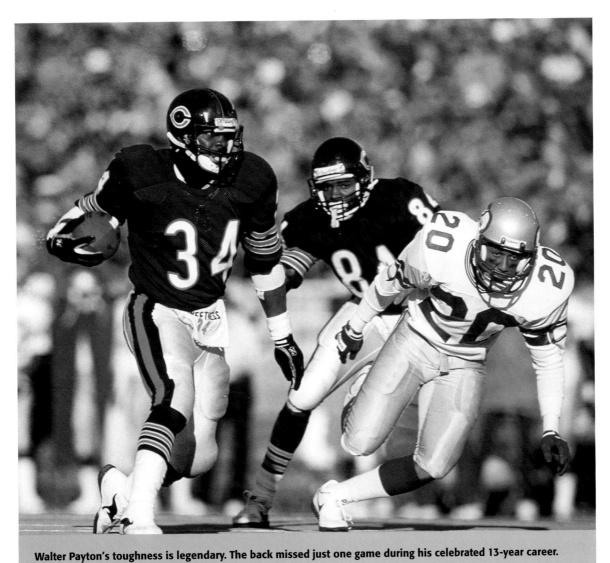

Walter Payton's toughness is legendary. The back missed just one game during his celebrated 13-year career.

auto racing team and power equipment company, he was still a solidly built 220 pounds.

And now he was announcing that he, like some 12,000 less physically gifted mortals around the nation, had a serious illness that could only be solved by receiving someone else's liver.

Those who knew him best, like onetime coach Mike Ditka, were convinced that, rare disease or no, Walter Payton would beat the rap. "If there's a way to beat it, he'll beat it, and be a great example for anybody who gets in dire circumstances," Ditka told Chicago sportswriter Don Pierson. "We've got to get him a transplant."

As the weeks went by, the news about Payton's condition was both bad and good. Reports showed the disease was progressing faster than expected, but then Payton, called "Sweetness" in his playing days, turned up to throw out the first pitch for the Cubs' home opener. He missed a previously scheduled convention appearance at McCormick Place because of fatigue, but managed to give a promised motivational speech to some Illinois businessmen by phone from his hotel near the Mayo Clinic, where he was receiving treatment.

Referring (in March) to the outpouring of support, he said, "For me,

Payton poured his heart and soul into every down, becoming the NFL's all-time leading rusher with 16,726 yards.

Payton's induction into the NFL Hall of Fame on July 31, 1993, was simply a formality, his bronze bust secured several seasons before his retirement in 1987.

Walter, with son Jarrett watching, shocks the world with the news that he has a rare liver disease and will need a transplant.

it's been uplifting. It's humbling. The reason I'm doing so well is because of the prayers that God has heard for me."

In May, still undergoing tests at Mayo Clinic that he hoped might move him up the donor list, Payton taped a Public Service Announcement promoting organ donation. The PSA was scheduled to run on CBS' "Touched By An Angel." "Walter didn't want to do something that came off sounding self-serving," Ginny Quirk, vice president of Walton Payton, Inc., told the Associated Press. "This gave him the opportunity to talk about the need for organ donation in a more general way."

Referring at the time to his day-to-day condition, he said, "Some days are better than others. You wake up

every morning and it's sort of like life: You don't know how you are going to feel."

The year before his illness changed Payton's reality, he had been visiting with Ditka in Wisconsin as the bristly coach and his New Orleans Saints were preparing for a game with the Bears. Ditka showed off shirts he had made, imprinted with the inspirational slogan, "Whatever It Takes." Payton pointed out, laughingly, that he had come up with the saying during his days with the Bears.

Now he needs to practice it again, against an opponent more serious than any football player.

"If we can get him back on even ground, he'll beat it," said Ditka, according to Pierson, about the player he once compared to only Jim Thorpe. "This is a great platform to tell people about organ donation. When you die, you can't take them with you."

Kirby Puckett

Blind Devotion

Kirby Puckett told us it wasn't really a sad day.

He reminded us of Rod Carew, the fellow Minnesota Twins legend, who had lost a daughter to leukemia. He told

us how his own family was healthy, except for the eye disease that forced him out of professional baseball but didn't slow him down otherwise one bit.

So why, then, on the day Kirby Puckett announced his retirement, were we all so full of grief? Probably because baseball (and, heck, all of sports) rarely sees a person such as Puckett.

Sure, he appeared in 10 All-Star Games. Twice he led the Twins to World Series championships. Of course, he won six Gold Gloves. But there have been other all-stars, other world champions, and many, many Gold Glovers.

There will never be another Kirby Puckett.

In an era in which players jump from team to team for the chance to add a few zeroes to the end of their paychecks, Puckett played for the Minnesota Twins for 12 seasons. He was fiercely loyal to a town that, as a whole, always had its attention divided between football and hockey, and to an organization that gave him a chance to

Kirby received the Roberto Clemente Man of the Year Award prior to Game 4 of the World Series in Atlanta, Ga., on Oct. 23, 1996. The award is presented each year to the player who best exemplifies the game of baseball both on and off the field.

Kirby never strayed beyond the Twin Cities area during a spectacular career that included 10 All-Star Game appearances, six Gold Gloves and two World Series championships.

Kirby's hope is that others will seek treatment for glaucoma before the disease destroys their eyesight, so along with the American Academy of Ophthalmology, Puckett has helped form a traveling educational series titled "Don't Be Blindsided."

play in the big leagues when it was desperate for anybody who could catch a ball in center field.

Even since his retirement, Puckett continues to make his presence felt. Along with the American Academy of Ophthalmology, he helped orchestrate "Don't Be Blindsided," a traveling educational series that encourages the public to visit a qualified eye care professional on a regular basis. It was glaucoma that ended Puckett's career so prematurely.

But that was well after Puckett, the product of the Robert Taylor housing projects (perhaps South Chicago's

Puckett stayed off tough Chicago streets as a teen, then became the consummate professional, serving as an example to kids everywhere.

The strong arms, lightning quick hands, double-barrel legs and heart were still willing, but Kirby's failing eyesight forced his early retirement in 1996.

roughest neighborhood), broke into Major League Baseball with four hits in his first game. That was after Puckett, who as a child stayed off the streets and did well in school, hit one of the most dramatic home runs in baseball history, an 11th-inning clout that won Game Six of the 1991 World Series.

That was after Puckett, the super-talented youngster who wasn't above taking advice from teammates and coaches, amassed a .318 career batting average, including a .314 mark his final year that proved he was nowhere near past his prime.

Then, too suddenly, it ended. During spring training in 1996, Puckett simply woke up one morning with a black dot obscuring the vision in his right eye. The dot eventually left, but the blurred vision didn't. After four months of tests and surgeries, Puckett announced that he was finished.

Then, during his retirement speech on July 12, 1996, Puckett reassured us. He told us everything was going to be OK. He was feeling good, and, at the age of 35, he had much of his life ahead of him.

For Kirby Puckett, it was a new beginning.

For the rest of us, it was a chance to reflect on a playing career that provided us with so many wonderful memories, and a chance to appreciate the fact that the Kirby Pucketts of this world don't come around often enough.

Cal Ripken Jr.

Pride of the Working Class

One man kept reality suspended for more than 16 years. Cal Ripken Jr. had been a constant in the Baltimore Orioles' box score since the second game of a 1982 doubleheader. That was until Sept. 27, 1998, when he chose to sit out the Orioles' last home game of the season. He wasn't forced out of the lineup because of an injury or poor performance; he did it on his own terms, making 2,632 baseball's new magic number.

In an era when multi-millionaire players sit out games because of blis-tered fingers and stubbed toes, Cal Ripken Jr. is a throwback. In 1995, the Baltimore Orioles' shortstop broke Lou Gehrig's 56-year-old record of 2,130 consecutive games played to become baseball's new Iron Man. Ripken's class and work ethic helped to win back fans

A Baltimore icon, Cal Ripken's dedication is a reflection of the city itself. A working-class town, citizens can easily relate to Ripken's unwavering work ethic and down-to-earth personality.

An autograph "Iron Man," Ripken has been known to sign for fans for hours both before and after games. When Cal Ripken signs an autograph he adds a "Jr." tail as respect for his father Cal Ripken Sr.

alienated from the game during the 1994 baseball strike.

Cal always will be linked with Baltimore and the Orioles. He played ball at Aberdeen High School in Maryland, worked his way through the Orioles' system, made it to the bigs and never left home.

During his career, Cal has been an icon and security blanket for the city. Baltimore is a tight-knit, working-class town that has been dubbed "the biggest small town in America." Cal Ripken Jr. is a reflection of the population of

Baltimore. When folks went to work at dawn and got home at dusk, they knew he'd be on the field ready to play — every day.

In the current MLB atmosphere of free agency and one-year contracts, Cal's devotion to his hometown and team are virtually unheard of. The Orioles are the city's team and Cal is the team's identity. He was a local boy and still is.

There were some fans who had never seen an inning of Orioles baseball without Cal in the infield. And when his streak hit 2,131 in 1995, he became even more ingrained in the fabric of the city and the Orioles.

His devotion to his city has extended to its charities. Cal and his wife, Kelly, have established the Kelly and Cal Riken Jr. Foundation that supports adult and family literacy and youth recreational programs in the Baltimore community. The Baltimore Reads Ripken Learning Center teaches 300 adults a year the fundamentals of reading, writing, math and computer skills. The Ripkens have helped raise more than $1.2 million for the center.

His dedication is also linked to his family. Cal teamed with his brother, Billy, in Baltimore for more than five years, and his father spent more than

Cal Ripken and his wife, Kelly, have worked tirelessly on charitable causes including establishing the Kelly and Cal Ripken Jr. Foundation, which supports adult and family literacy and youth recreational programs in the Baltimore community.

On the night of his record-tying 2,130th consecutive game, Ripken was given an opportunity to celebrate the occasion with New York Yankee legend Joe DiMaggio. The Yankee Clipper knew a thing or two about streaks of his own, having notched a hit in 56 consecutive games in 1941.

Before the move to third base in 1997 Cal Ripken had hit 345 career home runs and 855 extra-base hits as a shortstop. Both career numbers are tops among shortstops in major league history.

30 years in the Orioles organization as a player, third base coach and manager. In 1987 all three had the opportunity to contribute to the Orioles with Cal Jr. at

shortstop, Billy at second base and Cal Sr. as the manager.

When Cal signs autographs he adds a "Jr." tail as respect for his now late father, coach and friend, Cal Ripken Sr. On the night he broke Lou Gehrig's record he credited his father with teaching him his professionalism and loyalty. "He inspired me with his commitment to the Oriole tradition and made me understand the importance of it," Cal Ripken Jr. said. "From the beginning, my dad let me know how important it was to be there for your team and be counted on by your teammates."

Nolan Ryan

Lone Star Legacy

During his 27 years as a professional baseball player, Nolan Ryan used a simple plan against opposing hitters: throw three strikes. With a major-league record 5,714 strikeouts that helped make him an easy choice for induction into the Baseball Hall of Fame in 1999, Ryan's plan obviously worked.

And while he hasn't thrown strikes for a living since 1993, Ryan continues to lead his life through simple means: work hard, be determined, keep family values and do the right thing.

That's among the several reasons why he is a hero to people across the country, but especially in his home state of Texas, which looks upon Ryan as not only its unofficial ambassador, but also as the quintessential Lone Star native. Ryan is a small-town native with a big heart. His quiet dignity as a husband and father, a rancher, a banker, a humanitarian and a public official is a source of pride and inspiration for all Texans.

No wonder his nickname is "Big Tex."

"If you want to know the heart and mind of Texas, look at Nolan Ryan," Texas Gov. George Bush said the day Ryan was announced as a Hall of Famer. "He's as Texan as Texan gets — determined and hard-working. He loves his family. He's blessed with a can-do spirit that absolutely refuses to let obstacles stand in the way of any dream he has ever had. Nolan honed the talent God gave him into stuff of a baseball legend."

That legend continues to grow as Nolan leads his exemplary post-playing life. His love of the outdoors made him a natural fit to be appointed by Gov. Bush in 1995 to the Texas Parks and Wildlife Commission. Even though Ryan had no prior experience in state government,

A fearsome sight: standing in the path of a Ryan pitch. Nolan amassed a major-league record 5,714 strikeouts during a 27-year career.

Texans find it easy to identify with Nolan Ryan, a hard-working family man who gives total effort at whatever he does, whether it's throwing fastballs or herding cattle.

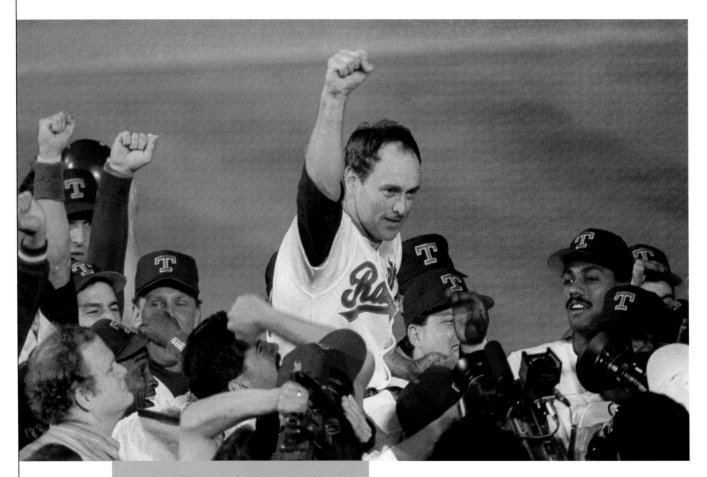

Ryan tossed a record-shattering seven no-hitters, the final gem coming for Texas against the Toronto Blue Jays on May 1, 1991.

he's earned respect for his attention to duty, which includes attending commission meetings and public hearings, visiting parks and promoting the TPW whenever possible.

"He's still throwing perfect strikes," TPW chairman Lee Bass told the Dallas Morning News.

He's also perfect for his hometown of Alvin, where he continues to live with his wife, Ruth. The Nolan Ryan Foundation funds scholarships, makes grants to charities and helped to open a continuing education center at the Alvin Community College. Nolan has never forgotten his small-town roots.

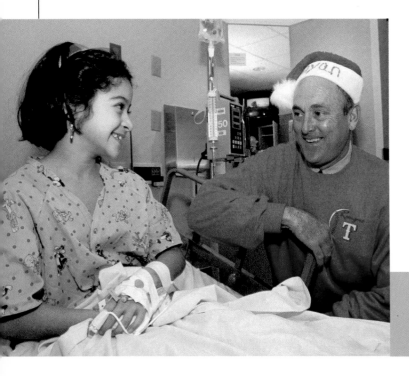

Ryan spreads holiday cheer to 8-year-old Cynthia Noris during a visit to Children's Medical Center in Dallas in 1995.

"If you want to know the heart and mind of Texas, look at Nolan Ryan. He's as Texan as Texan gets — determined and hard-working."
—Texas Gov. George W. Bush

And Nolan also has never forgotten the importance of doing the right thing — including good sportsmanship. Take, for example, the time in 1992 when Nolan saw a young flamethrower named Randy Johnson struggling with his mechanics. Nolan, who was playing for the Texas Rangers, offered some words of advice to the tall lefty, even though he was with the rival Seattle Mariners.

Johnson proceeded to have his breakthrough year in 1993, and is now one of the game's most intimidating pitchers. He credits Ryan with helping to turn around his career.

As is his nature, Ryan shrugged off the good deed. But his reputation as a do-gooder is matched only by his phenomenal pitching career. Consider what former major leaguer Rance Mulliniks once said when asked what kind of world it would be if everybody was like Nolan. Replied Mulliniks: "Everyone would love each other. And no one would get a hit."

Sammy Sosa

"Hero in Two Countries"

Perhaps the impact of Sammy Sosa's humanitarian efforts came to the forefront on Jan. 19, 1999, when he sat next to Hillary Rodham Clinton in the upper balcony of the House of Representatives, listening to President Clinton give his State of the Union address. Or perhaps it was when the President mentioned Sosa in his speech, calling the Chicago Cubs slugger "a hero in two countries."

Or perhaps it was at some other event, such as when he received a key to the city from Chicago mayor Richard Daly . . . or when he returned to his native Dominican Republic to be

Sosa handled the media onslaught associated with the great home run chase of 1998 with aplomb, even using the publicity to draw attention to problems in his native Dominican Republic.

honored with a "Day of National Celebration" and to receive his nation's highest honor, the Grand Cross of the Order of Duarte, Sanchez and Mella . . . or when he received the Medal of John Paul II during a special Mass at St. Patrick's Cathedral in New York.

You see, the importance of Sammy Sosa can't be defined by his 66 home runs, his MVP-winning season, or the rejuvenation he and Mark McGwire gave to baseball in 1998. Amazingly, his baseball talents — and they are considerable, to say the least — are overshadowed by his ceaseless desire to help the people, especially the children, of his native country. His fame as a baseball player provides him the stage to reach out for help, and never was that more important than 1998.

After Hurricane Georges ripped through the Dominican Republic in September, killing at least 283 people and leaving more than 100,000 home-less, Sosa quickly went on the offensive. He seemingly spent every available hour helping to solicit donations for the relief efforts, such as the $8,500 he received from Mayor Daly, the $15,000 he received from New York's Dominican community, and the $37,000 he raised in an auction during a base-ball tour of Japan.

"For me, raising money for my people at home is like a gift," Sosa told USA Today. "I know my people need help, and the only person they have who can come here to America and ask for help is me."

But his humanitarianism didn't just begin with his hurricane relief effort. Sosa has participated in many charitable causes the past few years. He spends much of his spare time at Wryler Children's Hospital in Chicago. In 1997, he organized a program called

New York City and mayor Rudolph Giuliani rolled out the red carpet for Sammy on Oct. 16, 1998, throwing a parade for the Dominican slugger and handing over a key to the city.

"Sammy Claus World Tour" that provided toys to more than 7,000 needy children in the Dominican Republic and the U.S. He's long donated Cubs tickets to less-fortunate children, and in 1998, he donated 40 computers to Dominican schools every time he hit a home run.

Meanwhile, The Sammy Sosa Charitable Foundation helps to raise the health standards in both his native country and his adopted U.S. Says Sosa: "Being with people and helping people is something I'm enjoying."

No wonder his agent, Tom Reich, calls his client a folk hero. "I've represented other MVPs and superstars," Reich also told USA Today, "but Sammy has taken it to a level that I haven't seen in 30 years."

That's true of both his baseball ability and his work for charity.

Gene Stallings

Straight Shooter

"You can't go wrong by doing right."

That was Gene Stallings' simple, yet appropriate reply recently when asked to contribute a line to the book, "The Most Important Thing I Know About the Spirit of Sport."

It could have been the answer to any of life's questions posed to Stallings.

The straight-shooting, Texas-born-and-bred coaching legend always has done it his way: the right way.

That was the case when at 29 he was the nation's youngest head coach at Texas A&M, and the Aggies struggled yearly to put a competitive team on the field. That also was the case when he coached in the NFL, both as an

Gene Stallings experienced many ups and downs, both on and off the field, during his college and NFL coaching career.

Gene and Johnny share a special bond, and serve as an inspiration for other families with Down syndrome children.

Gene's son, Johnny, accompanied his dad as he stepped out onto the Louisiana SuperDome turf before Alabama's national championship game against Miami on Dec. 30, 1992. The Crimson Tide won, 34–13.

assistant with the Dallas Cowboys and as a head coach with the St. Louis Cardinals where he failed to build a winning tradition during a short, four-year span. And that was the case when Stallings took over the head coaching duties at Alabama, where he once served as a Bear Bryant assistant, and endured an 0–3 start.

But Stallings' no-nonsense, never-compromise coaching style paid off three years later when he led the tradition-rich Tide to an 11th national title, capping a perfect season with a 34–13 victory over Miami in the Sugar Bowl.

All the while, Stallings also was determined to do right off the field with his family. He married his high school sweetheart, Ruth Ann, immediately following his senior season at Texas A&M, and the couple soon celebrated the birth of two healthy daughters.

Eager to have a son who would follow in his footsteps and carry on the family name, Stallings was blessed with the birth of John Mark Stallings in 1962. But John Mark was born with Down syndrome, and the hard-driving coach was faced with a whole new set of challenges.

At first refusing to accept his son's condition, Stallings quickly learned to love and care for John Mark. He rejected pressure by friends and colleagues who suggested that John Mark would be better off institutionalized. He learned to accept that others would be uncomfortable, and even cruel, when seeing his son.

Then he became an inspiration to other families with Down syndrome children, penning the bestseller "Another Season: A Coach's Story of Raising an Exceptional Son."

When the responsibilities of being an NFL or major-college coach kept Stallings away from his family, his family often came to him. John Mark became a familiar sight around the locker room and coach's offices as he and his father shared time for snacks and other moments throughout each day. And the two tugged at a nation's heartstrings with their United Way commercials during Stallings' NFL stint.

Also born with a heart condition that prevented proper oxygen flow to the blood, John Mark wasn't expected to live past his first birthday. But the day Stallings led Alabama back to the top of the college football world, John Mark was there. He sat in on the pregame radio interviews and shared a private moment with his dad following the game.

Stallings said in his book that he remembers two things about that New Year's Day in 1992: how virtually no one had expected his team to walk away with the national title, and how "no one, not one doctor, not one friend, and certainly no one in our family, thought John Mark Stallings would live to be thirty years old."

All those years of doing right, both personally and professionally, had paid off.

Stallings went out a winner in Alabama, leading the Tide to a 17–14 victory over Michigan in the Outback Bowl on Jan. 1, 1997. Johnny's deteriorating health was reported as one reason for Gene's decision to call it quits.

Pat Head Summitt

Not Your Average Coach

It takes a special kind of athlete to play for Summitt, an athlete whose willing to work hard both on the court and in the classroom.

You don't necessarily have to be a basketball devotee to know the face.

That face, the one that's home to one of sport's most famous scowls. The one that's prowled the sidelines of women's collegiate basketball games for more than 25 years, and that recently has turned up in bookstores across the country and on TV magazine shows such as "60 Minutes."

The face belongs to Pat Head Summitt, longtime coach of the University of Tennessee Lady Volunteers, one of the winningest coaches in collegiate history, and just maybe one of the best coaches ever. And if the face transmits a scowl so intense it might tempt an errant player to go in search of someone more friendly, someone such as, say, Bobby Knight, it just as often reflects the glory of victory and accomplishment. Either way, it's a face Pat Summitt has earned.

Summitt grew up in the '60s, starting to play high school basketball in 1966, but she can hardly be called a child of the '60s. The '60s, after all, were laid-back and mellow; Pat Head's family was anything but. The '60s were

Behind Summitt's menacing scowl is a caring teacher who wants nothing but the best effort and results from her pupils.

the time the culture was learning how to party, and party hard. The Head family, meanwhile, was on the family dairy farm in a Tennessee backwater, working. And working hard. All the time. "We raised tobacco and corn and pretty much all our food," Summitt told USA Weekend in 1998, as her Lady Vols were beginning their march toward an unprecedented third consecutive women's NCAA championship.

When Pat and her siblings (three older brothers and one younger sister) weren't plowing fields or milking cows or driving a tractor, they learned bas-

ketball on a makeshift court their father constructed in the hayloft of their barn. It was a rough learning environment, as the three older boys gave no quarter to their younger sister. But, of course, Pat Head was not the type who needed any charity. She was treated, and acted like, the fourth son in the family, and her basketball skills, not to mention her physical and mental toughness, grew.

After playing through high school and college, Summitt was good enough to co-captain the first women's Olympic team to a silver medal in 1976. By then she had already begun her coaching

Tennessee 68, Old Dominion 59: Pat and son Tyler celebrate the Lady Vols' fourth NCAA title in 1996.

"I've always said, 'Teams may beat us, but they better not outwork us. Coaches may beat me, but they better not outwork me.'"
— Pat Summitt

career, taking the women's basketball coaching job at UT's main campus in 1974, the year Title IX kicked in, requiring equal athletic opportunities for women.

It wasn't exactly a high-profile or high-budget position, with the purchase of uniforms dependent upon doughnut-sale revenue and recruiting efforts amounting to hanging fliers in the girls' dorms. Fifty people showed up to see the team lose its first game by one point.

But it was a start. And the coaching principles she would live her career by (mainly playing by the rules), and the hard, hard work she learned from her family, were evident from the beginning. "I've always said, 'Teams may beat us, but they better not outwork us,' " Summitt told the Knoxville News-Sentinel. " 'Coaches may beat me, but they better not outwork me.' "

By 1984 she was good enough to have coached the 1984 women's Olympic team to a gold medal. NCAA championships occurred in 1987, 1989, 1991, 1996, 1997 and 1998. Her team's home game attendance grew to more than 8,000, and the women's basketball budget passed the $1 million level. (Summitt's base salary by 1996 had grown to $135,000, reportedly higher than that of any other UT coach.)

Best of all, perhaps, was the graduation rate gained by her players who completed four years' eligibility: 100 percent. "I don't want average people," she told USA Weekend. "Average people cut corners. Winners know there are no shortcuts."

Summitt and star Chamique Holdsclaw produced many happy moments, including three consecutive national championships, during Holdsclaw's time at UT.

J.C. Watts

Natural Born Leader

There are plenty of athletes who have made the move from sports to politics — Jack Kemp and Bill Bradley are just two who come to mind — but none in recent times can match the story told in the life of J.C. Watts. A renowned University of Oklahoma quarterback, Watts led the 1981 Sooners to a Big Eight championship and ensuing Orange Bowl victory.

After graduation, Watts first segued to a five-year pro career in the Canadian Football League. He followed that up by a return to Oklahoma in 1987 and entry into local politics two years later. Within five years of entering the political fray, Watts found himself a newly minted U.S. Congressman, elected the pivotal year (1994) that Newt Gingrich led a new Republican

majority into the U.S. Congress for the first time in more than 40 years.

Watts was right with him, for as a Republican (the second black Republican to win a seat in the House in 60 years), a member of the Christian Coalition, and an outspoken conservative, he was a high-profile member from the start.

Given a forum by the Republican leadership in part to encourage greater minority interest in the Republican Party, Watts excelled. By 1996, he had become a national figure. Watts spoke before the Republican National Convention that nominated Bob Dole and Jack Kemp.

"I'm thrilled Bob Dole has chosen the second best quarterback in the Republican Party, Jack Kemp, as his running mate," he said, needling Kemp on the subject of football. Then he gave the Republican response to President Clinton's 1997 State of the Union message.

J.C. helped lead the Sooners to the Big Eight championship in 1981 before testing his skills on a much different field of play.

Texas Gov. George W. Bush and his wife, Laura, pose after a news conference in 1998 in which they introduced Watts, Dr. Condi Rice, right, and Michigan Gov. John Engler, far left, as members of Bush's presidential exploratory committee.

Watts greets, Julie, a client at the alcohol and drug rehabilitation facility Keystone Hall in Nashua, N.H., in 1998. Watts was in New Hampshire to lend support to other state Republicans.

NATIONAL MINORITY POL
GAZINE
"A Different ... int on National Issue
1-...-5454

Watts' political career has been on the fast track since 1994 when he became just the second black Republican to win a seat in the House of Representatives in 60 years. Here Rep. Watts speaks to the 1996 GOP convention in San Diego in 1996.

In 1998, as heads rolled among Republican congressional leaders, Watts gained a prestigious spot in the House Republican leadership.

It was all pretty heady stuff for a man who was born poor in a small town in rural Oklahoma. "Never in their wildest dreams," said J.C. in an interview with the Toronto Star, "did Buddy and Helen Watts think the fifth child born to them, in a poor black neighborhood in Southeastern Oklahoma, would someday grow up to serve in the United States House of Representatives. I am the first black Republican to be elected south of the Mason-Dixon line since Reconstruction. It's obvious I did not win because of my skin color [Watts' district is majority white] or my party affiliation [his district is majority Democrat]."

Raised as a Democrat by his father, a preacher, policeman and ardent Democrat, Watts said that one of the most difficult things about entering politics was admitting to his father that he had switched political allegiances.

"I faced the awesome task of calling my father and saying to him, 'Dad, I am today a Republican,'" J.C. said. "I think I was probably more afraid of telling my father of this Damascus road experience than I was of ever facing any linemen in all of my football career."

But then, for a man who was named Julius Caesar Watts, political courage, even in the face of family opposition, should not be too surprising.

Pat Williams

Still Livin' Large

Pat Williams sounds as if he's taking a page out of the playbook of Auntie Mame when asked what people should learn from his life. "My message," he says, "is to live your life with passion. Live large. Don't get to the end and have regrets; don't end up saying 'I shoulda, coulda, woulda.' Take every opportunity and live life to the fullest."

There's no doubt that Williams, a longtime sports executive, motivational speaker, author (of nearly 20 books), and father (of 19, yes, 19 children) has been living life to the fullest. About the only goal he never realized — and this is a very goal-oriented person — was to become a major league baseball player.

"The author John Ruskin said, 'There is no wealth but life.' To live your life to the fullest, though, you've got to know what you want to do, and I've known since the age of 7 that I wanted to be involved in professional sports.

"My Dad took me to a Philadelphia Athletics baseball game in 1947, and I was overwhelmed by the whole ballpark experience — the crowds milling about, the smell of the hot dogs and peanuts, the tractor out working on the field. I loved the pageantry of it all, and I immediately knew I wanted to spend my life in sports, to play in the major leagues."

As it turned out, Williams lacked the baseball talent required to play in the major leagues, but he did achieve his goal of a life in sports. A baseball scholarship got him through Wake Forest University. A catcher's job for the Class A Miami Marlins quickly gave way to front office jobs both with the Marlins and the Spartanburg (SC) Phillies.

When Pat Williams says to live your life to the fullest, he knows what he's talking about. Williams has worked tirelessly as a sports executive, author, motivational speaker — and father to 19 children.

Pat and Ruth Williams managed to round up all 19 teen-agers for this wedding day photo on April 5, 1997.

Williams, who helped build the successful Orlando Magic NBA franchise from the ground up, has authored several books, including "The Magic of Teamwork," based on the eight qualities of successful teams.

In 1968, he switched sports professionally, becoming first the business manager of the Philadelphia 76ers, then the General Manager of the Chicago Bulls. He was just 29. After four years he went on to GM jobs with the Atlanta Hawks (one year) and the 76ers (12 years, including a World Championship title in 1983). In 1986 he went on to the Orlando Magic, where he currently serves as Senior Executive Vice President.

A successful career in sports and marketing, however, is only half the story of this remarkable man. He is the father to 19 children, 14 of them adopted. Unlike his life in sports, though, which was clear to him at a young age, his life as a father took a less direct route.

"Professionally, I'm living proof, as Steven Spielberg says, that dreams can come true," Williams says. "But one of the dreams I never anticipated was being the father of all these children," says Williams. "My first wife started wanting to adopt children from other countries almost immediately after we got married in 1972. I had no interest, though, and for 10 years refused to consider it. I felt I was too busy with work, and that I couldn't love a child that wasn't my own."

In an effort to save a marriage that had begun to fail, Williams changed course, and in 1983, he and his wife adopted two girls from South Korea.

"That opened the floodgates," says Pat. "Over the next 10 years we adopted 12 more — two more from Korea, four from the Phillipines, two from Romania, and four from Brazil. We didn't have any master plan about what we were doing; we didn't anticipate the tremendous costs, or the fact that we would one day have 16 teen-agers at one time. We just did it. I sensed God's leading hand.

"I got so caught up in adoption that I wanted even more children; we could have had as many as 30. But God closed those doors, which turned out to be a blessing."

After a 1997 divorce from his first wife, Williams married his current wife, Ruth, whose one child was the last addition to the combined family. Ruth teaches time management seminars for the Franklin Covey Company, a skill that must come in handy for such a complicated family, a family that recently had five members graduate from high school.

"It hasn't been easy," says Williams. "We live paycheck to pay-check, book to book, speech to speech. But if I believe anything, it's that there's a God of second chances — that He never gives up on us — and that it's during the bad periods when we grow the most.

"You know, the late Bill Veeck, whom I admired greatly for his ability to 'live large,' was eulogized in the Washington Post [by Thomas Boswell] with the phrase: 'Cause of death — life.' I would simply urge anyone who listens to me that we should all be able to have that on our tombstones."

Pat teamed with Mickey to author the 1995 book "Go for the Magic," based on Disney's five secrets of success.

Ricky Williams

At Second Glance

His dreadlocks, tattoos and earrings might lead many to roll their eyes and label the 1999 Heisman Trophy winner a rebel, someone with no respect for responsibility and authority. But nothing could be further from the truth.

In 1998, Ricky Williams listed as his lifetime goal to be an elementary school teacher. He also used a $50,000 signing bonus from the Philadelphia Phillies to help put his sisters through college. (He was drafted out of high school by the Phillies and played in their minor league system during his summers in college.)

In an age when most college athletes jump at the first chance to make

Ricky Williams ran away with the Heisman in 1998, rushing for 2,124 yards and 27 touchdowns. He also found time to smash some notable NCAA career records: yards (6,279), scoring (452 points), touchdowns (75) and all-purpose yards (7,206).

Ricky Williams wore No. 37 in the Texas/Oklahoma game at the Cotton Bowl, to honor his fallen friend, Doak Walker. After scoring a touchdown in the 34–3 romp he pointed both index fingers to the sky and said quietly, "This is for you, Doak."

Williams figured to be the target of Nebraska's swarming defense in the 20–26 Texas upset of the No. 7 Cornhuskers. But Williams gave the vaunted Blackshirts a black eye, carrying 37 times for 150 yards. In a sign of respect, the Nebraska fans applauded Ricky Williams after the game.

millions in the professional ranks, Williams stayed for his senior season — despite the certainty of being a top draft pick his junior year. He went on to set

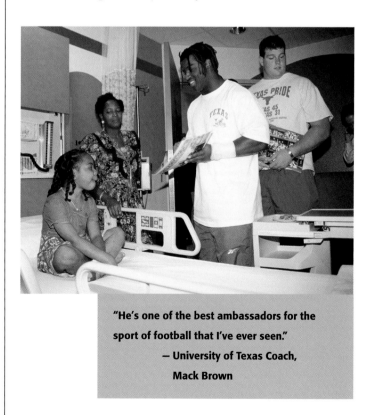

"He's one of the best ambassadors for the sport of football that I've ever seen."
— University of Texas Coach, Mack Brown

or tie 16 NCAA records and 44 marks as a running back at the University of Texas, leading the team to a 9–3 season that included a Cotton Bowl victory.

Williams, an education major, said he returned for his senior year so he could be a positive role model by encouraging kids to stay in school. He served as a mentor at Austin, Texas, elementary and middle schools and regularly visited patients at Austin Children's Hospital. In addition, he served as a spokesman at local schools in the Longhorn Crime Stoppers program.

After winning the Doak Walker Award in 1997, Williams became friends with the legendary Walker himself. The two remained close and kept in contact throughout the year, the veteran giving Williams advice about life both on and off the field. When Walker died after a tragic skiing accident, a devastated Williams dedicated his final record-breaking college season to him.

For the annual Texas-Oklahoma game played in the Cotton Bowl (also known as the house that Doak built), Williams changed his jersey number from 34 to 37, the number of the former SMU great and 1948 Heisman Trophy winner. After a fourth-quarter touchdown, Williams pounded his jersey and pointed both index fingers to the sky and said, "This is for you, Doak." Williams ran for 139 yards and two touchdowns in a 34–3 domination of the Sooners.

After the game, the team gave the game ball to Walker's family. While presenting the ball to the eight members of the Walker clan, Williams decided to add something of his own.

"Ricky took off his dirty, sweaty jersey with blood on it and quietly gave it to the family in Doak's honor," remembered Texas head coach Mack Brown. "And as tears were in his eyes and everyone else's, Ricky said, 'Sorry about the blood and mud.' But that's just Ricky." Williams continued to wear a No. 37 decal on his helmet for the rest of the season as a tribute to his friend.

Williams became college football's all-time career leading rusher in a nationally televised, final regular-season game against Texas A&M, Texas' biggest rival. The man who had held the record for 22 years, Tony Dorsett, watched from the Texas sideline.

"If someone is going to break the record, I'd rather see it done by a class act like Ricky," Dorsett said. "You can't help but root for him."

The record-breaking performance made him a lock for the Heisman. The fact that he won it on the 50th anniversary of Doak Walker's Heisman win added special meaning to the honor. With the largest margin of victory in the history of Heisman Trophy voting,

The New Orleans Saints traded every single 1999 draft pick they owned , along with two picks next year, to move up into position to draft Williams. Saints coach Mike Ditka suggested it was divine intervention that led Ricky to New Orleans.

Williams, true to form, turned college football's ultimate individual prize into a team triumph.

"The knock on me winning the Heisman Trophy at the beginning of the year was that I wouldn't play on a team good enough for me to win it," Williams said. "But my teammates came through, and I share this award with them."

CHARITIES

The athletes and coaches in this book have supported one or more of the following charities:

Special Olympics, Inc.
1325 G Street, NW Ste. 500
Washington, DC 20005
(www.specialolympics.org or
www.99game.com)

Racing for a Reason
c/o the Leukemia Society of America
North Carolina Chapter
5624 Executive Center Dr., Ste. 100
Charlotte, NC 28212
(www.jeffgordon.com)

Glaucoma Research Foundation
200 Pine St., Ste. 200
San Francisco, CA 94104
(www.glaucoma.org)

The Doug Flutie Jr. Foundation for
Autism
c/o The Giving Back Fund
54 Canal Street, Ste. 320
Boston, MA 02114
(www.dougflutie.org)

The Troy Aikman Foundation
1000 Ballpark Way, Ste. 302
Arlington, TX 76011

The Page Education Foundation
P.O. Box 581254
Minneapolis, NM 55458-1254

Crime Stoppers International, Inc.
P.O. Box 30413
Albuquerque, N.M. 87190-0413
(www.c-s-i.org)

The Walter Payton Foundation
(www.payton34.com or www.unos.org)

Kelly and Cal Riken Jr. Foundation
2330 W. Joppa Rd., Ste. 333
Lutherville, MD 21093

The Sammy Sosa Charitable Foundation
c/o The Chicago Cubs
1060 West Addison St.
Chicago, IL 60613

United Way of America
701 N. Fairfax St.
Alexandria, VA 22314-2045
(www.unitedway.org)

WRITERS

Joel Brown, who contributed chapters featuring Grant Hill and Gene Stallings, is an associate editor for Beckett Publications.

Aaron Derr, who contributed chapters featuring Mark McGwire and Kirby Puckett, is an associate editor for Beckett Publications.

Tracy Hackler, who contributed the chapter featuring Terrell Davis, is a senior editor for Beckett Publications.

Greg Holzhauer, who contributed chapters featuring Tim Duncan, Cammi Granato, Mia Hamm, Michelle Kwan, Mario Lemieux, Casey Martin, Paul Molitor, Mercury Morris, Alan Page, Walter Payton, Pat Summitt, J.C. Watts and Pat Williams, is a Dallas-based freelance writer.

Rucy Klancnik, who contributed chapters featuring Jim Abbott and Troy Aikman, is editorial director of Beckett Publications.

Mike McAllister, who contributed chapters featuring Nolan Ryan and Sammy Sosa, is a managing editor for Beckett Publications.

Alan Muir, who contributed the chapter featuring Adam Graves, is a senior editor for Beckett Publications.

Mike Pagel, who contributed the chapter featuring Doug Flutie, is an associate editor for Beckett Publications.

Tim Polzer, who contributed chapters featuring Cris Carter and Cynthia Cooper, is executive editor of Beckett Publications.

Brian Richardson, who contributed chapters featuring Cal Ripken Jr. and Ricky Williams, is an associate editor for Beckett Publications.

Mark Zeske, who contributed the chapters featuring Jeff Gordon and Ernie Irvan, is a senior editor for Beckett Publications.